My Journey to Peace with PTSD

Lady Cerelli

Peace with PTSD Organization™

Peace Publishers
P. O. Box 668
Hot Springs, NC 28743
www.PeaceWithPTSD.org

Front cover art designed by Lady Cerelli
Author's Photo by Peggy DeBell
Cover & Interior layout designed by J. L. Saloff
Fonts: Adobe Caslon Pro, President, Market

The names of the chapters came from history and language of flowers from www.VictoriaBazaar.com.

The poem *Survivor Psalm* by Frank Ochberg, MD & Gift From Within was used with permission.

First Edition

Cerelli, Lady
My Journey to Peace with PTSD

10-Digit ISBN: 0-9798883-0-1
13-Digit ISBN: 978-0-9798883-0-4
LCCN: 2007935188

Printed on Acid Free Paper in the United States of America

**Names of certain individuals have been changed to protect their privacy.*

1.0

Praises for My Journey to Peace with PTSD

Lady's depiction of her journey from childhood trauma to adult well-being illustrates the reality of what it is like to live with PTSD and what it takes to recover. This is a movingly written book which educates the reader as to why children who have been harmed continue to be vulnerable in adulthood. Lady very frankly shares how the body-mind mechanisms for survival and self-protection can result in painful and maladaptive behaviors long after a traumatic event.

Lady writes with extreme tenderness toward the child she was, who still exists within her. This book will validate and inspire other survivors of PTSD on their own journeys toward peace, and be a resource for those who love them.

Irene J. Libretto, LCSW

The compelling account of Ms. Cerelli's abuse, beginning as a young child, is raw and uncensored. When you read of her abuse as a child, you'll see she has the ability to put the reader back in time to experience the feelings of a confused and betrayed little girl. Her loss of innocence is painful and palpable.

As she journeys you through her life, you experience the roller coaster of mental illness that plagues her because of her severe trauma and her suppression of pain, rage and memories. She brings the reader to an understanding of how her repressed rage bubbles to the surface, and manifests in her many self-destructive behaviors.

Although reading Ms. Cerelli's reliving of her abuse is excruciating at times, she mentions the people in her life, mostly women, who gave her "just enough" to carry her through her survival. She is a strong woman who continues to fight back with every trauma.

Just as you experience her tortuous ride through her abuses, you are carried along through her journey of healing. When she plants her garden, works with the Earth and the plants...they begin to heal her. Mother Earth, with her unconditional love, nurtures her back, and she is able to move forward.

The book is filled with the creative ways Lady uses her positive coping skills to survive. I think, along with hope, this is the greatest gift she gives the reader. She chose to survive! I believe that with hope and "just enough," anyone can survive. Anyone who has experienced any type of trauma will greatly benefit from her compelling story of survival.

Dr. *Terry J. Apt, ARNP-C, N.D.*
Doctor of Naturopathy,
Holistic Nurse Practitioner

For my husband:
For his courage and strength in staying with me for
forty-two years, and for teaching me what love is.
Baby, we're finally getting it right.

Table of Contents

Foreword

by Ruth Crawford, LCSW, ACSW

Dir. of Mental Health Services for Military Sexual Trauma,
James H. Quillen VA Medical Center

If there is one thing that I've learned while working with trauma survivors for over twenty years, it is that they have very mixed feelings about focusing on their trauma in any way. Many, such as the author of this book, have little choice in the matter as they unintentionally lose the memory of what happened to them. Others make a conscious decision to try to put the trauma and resulting pain behind them. When a victim of trauma cannot or does not face what has happened, she tends to respond to life in a way that is puzzling to her and others. Avoiding the memories can take on many forms: alcohol or drug abuse, working long hours, sexual acting out, perfectionism; the list is endless. Numbing of emotions often accompanies this avoidance, for to feel the horror all over again is far too painful for a victim to imagine. The problem is that the avoidance and emotional numbing can take a terrible toll on a victim's life. Additionally, it doesn't work. Trauma makes itself known in various subtle and not-so-subtle ways. It emerges in dreams, in flashes of memory, and in emotional overreaction; it defines its victims' fears and prejudices. It tugs at its victims' consciousness, often rendering them unable to clearly focus on the life they are trying to live. And it undermines the spirit.

When a trauma victim consciously decides to face what happened to her, she begins the long and often painful journey to becoming a survivor. As the author has so clearly recognized, the journey cannot be undertaken alone. The effects of trauma thrive in secrecy and shame. Freedom from its bonds can only be attained by sharing one's experiences and reactions. While this process is arduous and often lifelong, the benefits are many. The trauma victim-turned-survivor can, by putting the pieces of the past together, attain a sense of wholeness previously unknown to her. She can come to accept the reality of what happened to her and how it may have altered her life, and make informed choices about how she wishes to continue living her life.

In *My Journey to Peace With PTSD*, Lady Cerelli documents for the reader the path that she took to become a trauma survivor. More than that, she documents her entire life story, putting her trauma into historical perspective. In doing so, Ms. Cerelli also, as psychologist Yael Danieli states it, "recreates the flow" of her life and restores a sense of continuity with the past. Through this process, she reclaims her life and her sense of personal power. And by sharing her story, Ms. Cerelli brings meaning to her struggle by showing the reader that he or she can also become a survivor.

Her courage is remarkable, and testimony to us all.

*

Author's Note

Journaling my life was not easy. I can't tell you how many times I went into depression, swore at things and people, got in the car and drove (mostly my husband drove), and simply sat outside to let my mind wander, or sat with my dog. And let's not forget the times of frustration when, with my friends, my mouth stepped in front of my brain because I couldn't stay focused on the moment. My friends are truly kind.

My biggest lesson, since the flashback, was my finally understanding why *"No man is an island, entire of itself..."* No one makes a decision alone or stands alone. Decisions are always based on someone or something. It may be a color, a statement, a number, or something seen or heard—anything can affect any kind of decision. Indeed, humans were made to be with others, to share trials and celebrations. This is the reason I wrote my most intimate, embarrassing, dysfunctional life in the way I'm presenting it now. You need to know: you are not alone; how abuse in childhood presents itself in adulthood; and that no abuse of any kind should be tolerated.

I've talked to Guidance since I was four and still do today. I'm not schizophrenic—I've checked. Don't think I acquiesce more easily with age; we still argue, and I will always have questions. In the end, I obey, much to my husband's chagrin. But even he doesn't argue anymore because he's witnessed too many occasions when Guidance has been right.

As a spiritual counselor, I've never hung out a shingle and never advertised. Since I was twenty-one, there has been a steady stream of people in need of counseling, but I've never had more than I could handle while taking care of a home and maintaining a full-time job. Though the sessions were generally in my home, I have gone to the client on occasion. Sometimes the sessions are two hours long for one visit; other times I see them for two or three years. I have even stayed in a clients' home if I knew they were approaching the critical time and that if someone wasn't with them, they would revert back—as was the case with a woman with low self-esteem who was getting out of an abusive relationship.

Though there are as many healing modalities in all cultures and races of people as (wo)man's imagination will allow, my method has been created with the help of my clients, my teenage foster children, my own intuition and scenarios, and other professionals. But, mainly, it came from sitting down with the individuals, getting into their pain, and then pulling out what they needed to guide them on their healing path. Diversity of the human psyche stemming from life experiences, geographical locations, sociology, and levels of intellect is too vastly complicated for me to label with specifics or to draw on 'casebook' examples. Rather than slotting people by behavior patterns, or dissecting their mentalities, I look at them as a whole entity and help guide them to connect the dots in their mind, body language, and behaviors by taking them back to the beginning and bringing them forward.

This kind of mental processing is rarely done alone with much success. You need to share your hurt and *not* give it strength by keeping it to yourself. Believe me, with the same certainty that if a rock is dropped it will hit the earth, you are not the only one who has been abused by a loved one or close family member, or raped, or… I have not met anyone in all my years that has not been touched in some way or another by sexual abuse—even if just through knowing someone.

This book depicts abusive scenes in graphic detail, because I feel our society has gone too far in sweeping abuse under the carpet, into closets, or downplaying it for sensitive ears. On the other end of the scale, I am also aware that anesthetizing it with too many graphic scenes can desensitize our society—truthfully, I feel we've done that anyway through the media. As I try to create balance with my clients, I have tried to balance the negative and dark parts of this book by relating significant and positive episodes in my life—those things that have sustained and still sustain me.

My story or my suggestions are in no way intended to diagnose anyone's mental health or state of mind and is not to be construed as such. Nor does any one method work as a one-size-fits-all solution. If any part of this book resonates with you to the point of pain, for the love of yourself and those in your life, go immediately to the nearest therapist. There are many of them out there with sliding pay scales, and the county mental health systems are usually free or have nominal fees. If you are not comfortable with that choice, please find a friend, a support group, or a buddy. Find *someone* to share your pain and help you through the process of healing.

There is no price for peace of mind.

Flashback

Seeing a blob of something on my studio floor tile, I reached for the paint scraper and bent to the task. And while I scraped, concrete seeped through and the tiles completely faded away before my eyes. I found myself scraping a concrete floor. *What the…? I have tiles on my concrete floor. Where are my tiles…?*

Confused and feeling nauseated, I stood up and looked around. I was no longer in my studio. Deep laundry sinks lined the side walls in a row, from the front of a thirty-foot laundry room to the back. I couldn't believe my eyes. *I remember this place. This is the laundry room in boot camp…! That was over 40 years.... Where is my studio?*

My body didn't move as the scenery around me shifted again and I stood on the quarterdeck in the WAVES barracks. A few seconds after that, shock registered; the door of the motel room appeared in front of me and my brain recognized its familiarity.

My heartbeat shot up to my throat, constricting my breath. My mind willed my hand not to move. My breathing laborious, I watched in horror, unable to stop it, as my hand reached for the doorknob. *I don't want to do this. Please God…!* I didn't understand my fear. How did I know what was behind the door? I didn't have to touch the door knob because in the next moment I was inside the room.

Every fiber of my being resonated with the odors. Moving my head, like a camera panning in slow motion, I scanned the room. The wallpaper was still old and made even more yellow from the light glowing through the tobacco-stained lampshade. Struggling hard, I fought not to look. *Close your eyes…close your eyes.* Sweat broke out on my forehead as I turned my head toward the bed. There was blood on the gold carpet, on the sheet draping off the bed, and a lot of blood on the body. My body. *My God! That's me! So much blood! Where did it come from? Is that my blood?*

I jumped back from the door as someone charged into the room and ran to the bed. "Lady, can you hear me?" the man asked.

I know him! Bile filled my throat. As the man gently rolled me over, sharp pains shot through my groin. I heard myself moan at the same time I moaned on the bed. The man quickly pulled the sheet over my naked body. *My God, my vagina hurts.* I held my abdomen as I dropped to my knees on the carpet. *I can't believe this pain.* Folded over my knees, I could smell the carpet. It stank of alcohol, urine, and mold. *What did he do to me?*

"Careful, BG, she's hurting. Where in the hell did all this blood come from?"

BG picked me up ever so gently and cooed to me like one would to a baby.

I opened my eyes and stared up at him. *I know you.* I lay in his arms half-conscious, seemingly between two worlds.

How can I be here, seeing myself and feeling myself in his arms at the same time? Am I in a parallel universe?

My brain wouldn't, couldn't register any more of the horror in front of me. I touched the floor to see if it was real. The studio floor tile reappeared through the image of the blood on the carpet, now fading and becoming transparent. The motel room disappeared and I was again in my studio, kneeling.

The tile felt cold and wet on my bare legs as I held onto my abdomen…scared out of my mind. *What the hell just happened? My vagina hurts so badly.* I smacked the floor with an open hand and a smarting pain shot up my arm, confirming my reality. It also reminded me of the pain in my groin, and I heard myself moan again. Moving cautiously, I looked to see if there was any blood on the tile. I saw none and the pain eased off a little.

My brain had a hard time registering the present. Part of it was still back in that room…. *That wasn't real. It was a nightmare and I'm going to wake up from it any minute now.* Grabbing hold of the shelf under the sink, I pulled myself up, my body feeling like someone had beaten me with a fist. Moving my grip on the edge of the sink, I sucked in deep, slow breaths while scanning the room for assurance that I was still in my studio. *The mop's still there. I spilled water on the floor again! Where's the paint scraper?* As if in answer to my question and seemingly of its own volition, my hand holding the paint scraper rose up in front of my face. *Had I ever let it go?* I dropped it now onto the sink counter and took unsteady steps toward the door. My insides quivered, more from fear than from the easing pain.

With each slow step, the pain in my vagina pain gradually disappeared. In the short distance between the studio door and my house, my mind reached back to conversations with Barb, her telling me I have PTSD and me telling her she was full of shit. "PTSD is for someone who has seen war. I haven't been in a war," I remembered saying. Now, I wasn't so sure. In the kitchen I picked up the phone and dialed. "Barb, this is Lady. You fill out the paperwork for the VA hospital and I'll pick them up this afternoon." Having worked for the Veterans Administration for several years, Barb had helped other veterans in with their paperwork.

"I can't take you tomorrow because I have another appointment. Can Jim take you?"

"No. Isn't there someone else?" *Why don't I want my husband to take me?* For just a hairsbreadth moment I sensed two of me in one body: One living in the present, and the other from the past saying things I didn't understand.

"I can ask Judy. She can keep a confidence. Are you all right?" Barb's voice told me she was worried.

"No I'm not, Barb. I entered into another time zone or something. It scared the shit out of me. My God, I can't believe how my vagina hurts. It's like he took a knife to it…and the blood."

She cut in with, "It was a flashback, Lady," and was breathless, almost excited.

I didn't want to believe her. "Barb, I'll pick up the papers up in a couple of hours. Okay?

My hands still shook as I dressed, all the while wondering if what Barb had said was true. *And why in the hell was she excited?* Going out to the car, I was grateful that my visiting grandson had left to go back to Michigan with his girlfriend, and my son was golfing with my husband. My hands on the steering wheel felt steady, but the fact was, I was scared, more frightened than I have never been in my life. Standing in front of Barb's door, I shook anew when I realized I didn't remember the drive over.

"Come in." Barb held the door open and looked me over carefully. "Are you okay?"

"Hell no! Never before in my life has anything brought me to my knees. What's frightening is that my vagina is still painful from what feels like a butcher's job" Remembering her breathless voice earlier, I demanded, "And would you mind telling my why the hell you were so excited on the phone."

"I wasn't excited. Well, I was, but.... I've been trying for a while to get you into the VA. I'm just glad you're finally going."

Barb had already filled out some of the information on the paperwork for the hospital. She helped her husband at the American Legion and knew most of the vets.

"What are they going to do to me there?" According to my discharge papers, I had been in a psychiatric ward twice while in the Navy, but never knew why.

"Whatever they have to."

"Not good enough, Barb. Talk to me."

"I don't know, Lady. They'll evaluate you, I'm sure." Before I could ask anything else, she handed me a paper to sign. "Don't forget your marriage license, too."

"Who's going to take me?" During the drive over to Barb's, it surprised me that, having gone down my short list of *friends* there wasn't anyone I could ask. In the seven years we had lived in these mountains, I had found no one in whom I could confide.

"Judy will pick you up at 8 a.m."

"Who's Judy?"

"She's the wife of another veteran and a good friend of mine. Don't worry! She's very good at keeping her mouth shut." Barb handed me the large envelope with a contact name on the front.

I shook my head at the idea of her knowing everyone, including those in the ER at the VA hospital.

"Good luck, Lady, and let me know how it works out."

In the next moment I stood in her garage. Fingering the envelope in my hand, I wondered at the speed of events since I had gotten out of bed that morning. Something told me I was on a downward, spiraling path and had no control over it. Alice in Wonderland going down the rabbit hole popped into my head.

✻

"Thank you for bringing me, Judy. For some reason I didn't want my husband to."

Why didn't I want Jim with me? Judy seemed nice as we talked during the hour and half drive. Within a couple of miles of the VA hospital, I became edgy and rubbed my sweat-slick hands against my thighs.

"Judy. I'm feeling a whole lot better. We can go back home, now." I heard the anxiety saturate my voice. "Really, I'm fine." I wasn't sure exactly who I was trying to convince.

Patting my arm, she cooed, "Sure you are. But since we are here why don't we go in anyway and see what they have to say? Okay?" She kept driving.

As we entered the ER, something inside of me came unglued. I did my best to hold it in place. My hand shook as I gave the envelope to the gentleman behind the desk.

Upon opening it, he read my name aloud. "Barb called me this morning."

Of course she did.

"Just have a seat in the waiting room and someone will be with you."

Sitting in the upholstered chair, something went off inside of me, a tiny explosion. *I can hold onto this. Stay calm. No one is going to hurt you.* My eyes filled, then a drop fell on my cheek.

Judy stared at me, "Are you all right?"

Patting her arm, or rather, it was more like my hand jerking as it touched her arm, I said, "Yes…No. I…I don't know, Judy." I was surprised that my voice was also shaking. "I can't stop what's going on…."

"Lady, will you come this way, please?" The nurse stood patiently as Judy helped me up. Both of us were shocked at my weakness. The three of us walked the short distance into a room off the hallway. The nurse took my vital signs: BP was 120 over 72; however, my pulse was 113. She asked a few questions about my health. Then she asked why I was there.

I explained what Barb had said was a flashback then said, "I'm fine. I want to go home," yet I remained seated.

She ignored me and said, "Everything looks fine, dear. Would you please sit there a moment while I go find a doctor?" She patted my shoulder before walking out the door. A few minutes later, she was back. "Well, dear, you're in luck. We have someone free to see you."

"I said I'm fine. I…I…wa-want to go home."

"Yes you are, but she'd like to talk with you. It will only take a moment." She guided me as we left the room and walked three more doors down. After knocking twice, we walked in. "Doctor, this is Lady." The nurse again patted my shoulder, which was beginning to irritate me, before walking out.

I wanted to yank open the door and run after her. I saw Judy was holding my purse and tried to remember when I had given it to her. *Things are moving too fast for my brain. I need some time here.* "You know, I feel so much better. I—"

The doctor cut me off, "Can you tell me about your flashback?"

I didn't like her. She was too curt. *But I can get out of this.* I gave her the highlights. When I reached the part about coming back into my studio, my body shook uncontrollably and I couldn't stop it.

"Do you have any suicidal tendencies?" Her question, asked while suddenly turning in her chair, startled me.

"No." I tried to sound calm, but my voice cracked. *I have to impress this doctor. I don't like the way she's watching me.*

"Do you have any homicidal tendencies?"

"You mean do I want to kill someone? Yeah! " *Is she for real?*

"Can you name them?"

"Yes."

"Will you give me their names?"

"What are you going to do with the information?" *She's in with them.*

"We won't do anything with the information. But if we feel their lives are in danger, they have the right to know."

It doesn't matter to me, lady. I gave her five names of local yokels.

"How would you kill them?"

"Line 'em up in a room and shoot 'em, one by one, between the eyes." *Actually, I want them to hurt first.*

"You sound like you have manic-depressive tendencies. Do you think you are manic-depressive?"

I had been answering her questions as fast as she had been shooting them at me, but I reined up on this one.

"I'm not manic…" But I couldn't finish. My voice quivered, my body shook. "I'm fine." I heard laughter and was shocked when I realized it was coming out of me.

It equally shocked me to see a black woman sitting ever so serenely in a chair just behind the doctor. She seemed to have appeared out of nowhere. Ignoring me, she looked off into the corner as though deep in thought. *What the hell's the matter with that bitch?*

Doesn't she see me, or hear me? Somebody help me, please. I don't know what's happening. I can't control anything. God...please. My hands suddenly covered my face.

Unintelligible words flew out of my mouth between bouts of anger and laughter.

"Lady, we're going to take you upstairs and admit you." *Yes, I can use a few days. I need time to figure out what is going on here.*

The black woman rose out of her chair and looked gently into my eyes. "Is it all right if I go with you?" She put a strong arm around my shoulder as we walked out the door. Judy still held my purse. *I forgot about you, Judy, I'm sorry.* I looked her in the eyes. She smiled at me. *I'm glad she's okay. I'm glad someone's okay.*

When did we get to the elevator? Where are we going? Tears came hard then shut off just as suddenly as we walked down the hall toward double doors. *Double doors! No, I'm, not going in there. I want to go home.* I tried to turn around to leave, but the black woman's arm held me firm.

"I know exactly how you feel." *You don't know shit, you bitch.*

"Three months ago I was right where you are right now. And look at me now. You are going to be okay, but you need to do this." Her arm was like a vice grip as we moved closer to the double doors.

"This is the psychiatric ward, isn't it?" I asked, trying my best to hold onto whatever dignity I had left.

If I hit her real hard, would I hurt her? I don't really want to hurt anyone.

"Yes. There are real nice folks in there and they're going to help you." She pressed a button. A bell rang on the other side of the doors followed by a loud buzzer just before the doors opened.

Fear rose into my throat as several people rushed toward us. Spastic tears came hard…then laughter again. In between breaths, I cried out, "I don't know what to do. Please tell me what to do," and I started crying again. "I don't want to do this."

A nurse jerked her head up from the blood pressure cuff. "We can't make you stay. You have a choice here."

No one moved…waiting.

"No, I don't. Look at me here." I raised my arms. *Help me, God. Please help me. I don't know what's going on. Is this what it's like to lose my mind?*

Taking the cuff off my arm, she stated flatly, "200 over 140," and stuck out her hand. Someone gave her a small package. Opening it she took out a tiny pill and handed it to me with a small paper cup of water that seemed to have appeared out of mid-air. "Take this. It will make you feel better."

I handed her the empty cup after swallowing the pill.

"We're going to take you to lockdown."

Panic rose up and dried my throat. This time nausea came with it and I wanted to vomit. "What is lockdown?" *Why are you locking me up? What have I…?*

"Honey," she touched my arm and guided me toward another set of double doors. "Lockdown is just a term. We don't lock you up or down really. It's a part of this ward where we can keep an eye on you for 24 hours. Someone is going to be here all the time."

Something's happening to my head. When did I stop crying? Is my head floating above my body? It struck me funny that my head might be floating all by itself. I smiled as I reached up to make sure it was still on my neck. The nurse gave me a knowing smile as we went through the double doors and passed rooms sparsely furnished with plain, straight-backed chairs and low twin beds…not hospital beds. We turned left at a glass-enclosed corner that I recognized as the nurse's station. I smiled, in spite of myself. I feel good. "I'm okay now."

"I know, sweetie." *I hate it when they call me that. It's so condescending.* I smiled. *Where are my clothes? When did I get undressed?* I lay down my head on the pillow and rolled onto my side. Pulling the sheet and blanket up to my chin, I surrendered to the black velvet of sedated sleep.

✳

Peony-Shame

Living in a government apartment complex built during the war, I spent my playtime watching snakes eat rats in the Michigan basements of the long apartment buildings. What few toys I had were shared with my siblings. There weren't many girls in the complex, but I rarely played little girl games anyway—I never understood the *fun* in playing grownup. I had no time to learn them and those I did learn seemed childish to me. As the oldest child, with one brother and five sisters, I washed real dishes; changed real diapers on real babies; and fed and bathed all of them. In contrast, the boys fascinated me more as I learned to play marbles, ride their bikes and climb trees. I did have a birthday party, though, with mostly girls—I think it was my sixth birthday. But it was the only party I had.

We rarely got new clothes. They came from whomever and wherever we could get them. And if they didn't fit, Mom would alter them as they were passed down from the largest to the smallest:

things didn't always move from the oldest to the youngest. When we were through wearing the fabric as clothing, it was cut into pieces for quilts. Many times when we would lie awake at night and look over the quilt in the moonlight and either remember or make up stories pertaining to each piece of fabric.

"Here's Bobby's shirt."

"Yeah, remember when he got that bloody nose? There's the blood stain." Someone would point to the faded spot on the fabric that had become part of a doll pattern's hat.

All of the kids were in one of the two bedrooms in our apartment. One sister slept with me in a double bed, the other three girls slept in another double bed, and our brother slept in a small child's bed. The other bedroom was for Mom and Daddy and my baby sister in her crib. There was also one small bathroom with a claw-foot tub and a tiny sink hooked to the wall, and a combo living room and kitchen, with an archway dividing the two rooms. These four rooms with no closets measured a 24' x 24' square in the middle of about eleven other apartments in a long building.

My siblings became my surrogate children from the time I first changed my two-year-old brother's diaper when I was four. From the time Mom brought the babies home from the hospital, I jumped in as the eldest and did what had to be done—needing few, if any, instructions. Throw in a set of twins and we actually had five in diapers at the same time for a couple of months.

Precocious is one word that described me as a child. Another description was goody two shoes, so named by my brother. I used to beat him up for that until one day he turned and landed one on my chin, knocking me on my fanny. I forgave him, though. I didn't blame him.

A brand new purple snowsuit was all I could recall before my fourth birthday. Fifty five years would pass before I could remember Daddy undressing me when I was four. He kept pressing down on my chest with one hand while undressing me with the other, all the while shushing me. He took my underwear off while we were on his bed and I remembered being scared and screaming. The purple snowsuit must have been my retributive gift.

We never saw much of my alcoholic stepfather. He was the natural father of my siblings. I was told my natural father came through the Kentucky mountains before Mom was fifteen. He told her God said for her to do a thing; she did. Nine months later I popped out of the chute and religion went out the window. Daddy became my stepfather when he and Mom married when I was less than a year old. Our ancestors were the Cherokees, and the mutt-mixture of Scotch-Irish-English-German with our roots in southern Kentucky. But Mom, Daddy, and I moved to Michigan a few months after the coal mines closed.

There were times I thought my stepfather weird but could never quite explain what it was. One time we kids were playing with a kitten by the coal bin in the alley. Daddy came out through the kitchen door laughing and swooped up the kitten saying he was going to eat it for his supper. He then ran tap water into a pot and placed the pot on the back burner of the stove. I consoled my brothers and sisters as they stood there screaming and crying while staring at the horror in front of them.

I had seen enough of his cruelty to become anesthetized but would throw him a hateful look. Only then would he stop and try to grab me, saying he was sorry. But I always got away from him. Daddy used to say and do other things that made us laugh but often frightened us at the same time. I watched as he hurt animals or said nasty things to people. When they looked hurt or angry, he laughed at them.

He and Mom never talked much, unless they were arguing. And there was never any affection between them, though Daddy sometimes gave me attention. Working for a while at a local bar and restaurant, Mom was given the responsibility of closing the bar on most nights, around 3 a.m. It was on one of those nights Daddy's friends came over; and I, at age seven, got to stay up late. I felt special when Daddy held me on his lap while he and his friends played cards. One of them protested when Daddy let me try his beer then laughed when I spat it out. It tasted disgusting.

Daddy was drunk by the time his friends left. When he shut the door behind them, he turned around and stared at me. His new demeanor made me nervous. He walked toward me and picked me up in his arms. He then walked to his chair and put me on his lap.

His words slurred, he asked, "Does Daddy's little girl want fifty cents?" I normally enjoyed being hugged, having gotten so few, but this one was different. His breath stunk of alcohol and cigarettes. *Fifty cents will buy me that notepad with money left for candy.* Mentally counting the candy I could get for the other kids with the rest of my money, I nodded my head.

"Come on," he said and carried me toward his and Mom's bedroom. Daddy had never carried me before and this was the second time in one night. It felt good, yet odd. I had slept with Mom before, but she had never carried me as Daddy was doing. I wasn't afraid because he was my Daddy. He stumbled into the bedroom and dropped me onto the bed. My first alarm. I heard him panting as he fumbled with his clothes in the dark. My heart raced, not understanding my fear. In a few moments, the bed shuddered and groaned as his weight fell next to me.

He slurred "I love you" several times while slobbering on my face and fumbling with my nightgown. I deftly pulled the gown back down, growing more frightened when he roughly yanked it back up and growled, "Daddy's not going to hurt you."

Scared, I felt tears start to flow. He had never done anything like this before and I didn't know what to do. He pulled off my panties.

"Don't, Daddy. Please, don't." For a moment I had a terrifying thought that maybe this wasn't my Daddy in the dark, but the familiar stench of his breath confirmed the reality of the nightmare.

Forcing my legs apart, he tried to penetrate me, his breath rasping. The pain was incredible and I cried out loud, sobbing hard when he roughly picked me up while rolling over on his back. With his hand, he held the back of my head and shoved my face down onto his penis, forcing it into my mouth. The salty liquid of his instant orgasm gagged me and I nearly puked, tasting my blood. I didn't understand what I had done to be treated so roughly, or why he made me do these strange, hurtful things.

Thinking he was angry with me and not wanting to make him

angrier, I silently stifled my tears when he pushed me away. Getting off the bed, he staggered into the bathroom and vomited then turned around and shat, missing the toilet. He hollered for me to come in and clean it up. Like a good little girl, I did what I was told.

My broken heart ached. My chest full of painful disappointment also hurt from crying so hard. I had never before seen Daddy like this. I didn't know what I could have done to make him angry enough to physically hurt me and make me bleed where I pee-peed. I did everything he asked, but it wasn't enough. Savagely grabbing my arm, he snarled, "If you tell your mother, she'll get mad and hurt you. Now get your ass to bed." More frightened than I had ever been in my life, I ran like a scared kitten.

No one seemed to notice my not walking too well or the sudden onset of my dark moods. The pain between my legs subsided but was a constant reminder for several days. It hurt to wipe myself after using the toilet. If I happened to be in a room and Daddy entered, he would glare at me, daring me. Watching Mom I saw her stare at him with a hard expression on her face. Withdrawing within myself, I startled at the least noise. I stayed to myself or walked around the neighborhood after completing my chores; I didn't play much. When it finally occurred to me that I never got my fifty cents, I got mad and glared back at Daddy whenever he looked in my direction. I didn't hate him, but I didn't like him anymore, either. Daddy was rarely around after that and when he was, even my brothers and sisters felt the thick, smothering silence.

I never heard Mom and Daddy talk about love, nor did they ever say to us kids, "I love you." I was told whom to love and why:

"…she's your mother, your aunt, your sister…" But the word was never defined. I only knew my father was someone I was supposed to love, and who was supposed to love me. I began equating love with pain—in mind and body—because someone who is supposed to love me could hurt me and make me do strange things. Instinctively, I knew his actions were wrong. But sex never having been discussed in our home, I didn't relate it to sexual abuse. Not understanding the word sin, it never entered my mind, either.

I shared with my friend Elaine about what Daddy had done to our kitten, and about him taking me to bed with him and hurting me. She was my only friend and the youngest daughter of Mom's friend, Mary, who lived four apartments down from us. Elaine told me my father was sick in the head. I didn't understand why she would tell me he had a headache. And not liking her derisive tone, I didn't talk about him to her any more—or to anyone.

Confusion stayed with me and worsened when I remembered no cruelty to me before. Since there was very little communication in our household, I was left to my own thoughts. In my dark mood and with time alone, I convinced myself I had done something wrong and, therefore, deserved to be hurt. In the silence of unshared communication, this pattern of thought repeated itself over and over again. Eventually, I stopped wondering about things and thought my life was just the way it was. In fact, not having anything or anyone to tell me different, I believed it was the way every family behaved. So occasional odd behavior and mean streaks from Daddy became a natural thing.

Mom worked a lot of hours at work and even more at home;

she was tired all the time and always seemed angry. I didn't want her mad at me, so I did what I could to help her…in silence. Being the oldest of seven, I suspected Mom was in early pregnancy with her eighth child.

A few weeks later Daddy startled me out of a deep sleep in the early morning hours. Frightened, I became instantly awake when I smelled the alcohol on his breath as he again carried me out to the kitchen and put me on his lap. This time when he asked me if I wanted to earn fifty cents, I mutely stuck out my hand. Remembering not getting the money the last time, I felt brave at having conquered him when he put two quarters in my palm. I wasn't going to chance losing any money again and put out the other hand as I stared at him with tight lips.

Blushing, he hesitated only for a moment before putting two more quarters in my other palm. Hatefully, he stated, "I'll hurt your brother if you cry like a baby."

Like a good little girl, I did what I was told. I wondered why Daddy didn't wait for Mom and take *her* to bed. More often than not, I had the childhood fancy that a monster took over Daddy's body at those times. I began to notice other things about him and wondered what I had done for him to have changed so drastically. Sometimes I doubted these things happened in other families.

A week or two later we were in his bed for the third time. There were just threats this time, no "I love you" and no money. I tried my best to keep from breathing so I wouldn't to smell his breath. His body smelled bad, too, and he was impatient.

Then Mom walked into the room.

For an eternal moment the thunderbolt silence stopped my heart and Daddy's breathing while Mom froze in her tracks. In a flash and in one stride, she stepped over to the bed. With a hand of steel hand she hauled up my hefty body by one arm, and snarled, "Get your ass into your own bed."

I was shocked. Mom had never treated me roughly like this before. I was shocked further by again not knowing what I had done. Having raced back to my own bed, I lay there and listened to them arguing, using words I had never heard before.

Then silence descended—no noise of any kind.

My chest thumped harder and I held my breath. I didn't know what to expect as fear, like acid, filled my throat. In the hard silence, I heard a dresser drawer yanked open and slammed shut with such a loud force that my body jerked in bed. My curiosity got the better of me. I quietly slid out of bed, trying not to disturb my sister. At my bedroom doorway, I quietly dropped to my hands and knees, slowly twisted my upper torso, and peered around the partition into my parents' bedroom. I was certain they could hear my heart because it was beating so loudly.

The light from the alley shining through the dirty window silhouetted Mom pointing a handgun at Daddy as she said in a hard whisper, "Touch her again, I'll kill you."

The next day Mom would neither talk to me, nor look at me. My heart ached worse than my arm as I teetered on the verge of tears for most of the day. I didn't understand what made her angry with me. The morning hours dragged by and it was late afternoon when I finally found the courage to speak.

I patted Mom's arm to get her attention. "Mom, Daddy pees in my mouth when he takes me to bed with him." I wanted her to be as mad at him as she was with me.

She sat staring straight ahead as her lips tightened into a straight line. She was so quiet, I wondered if she had heard me. I touched her arm again, "Mom…"

Shrugging my hand away and responding in a tight, angry voice, she said "He didn't pee in your mouth. You just dreamed it."

Dumbfounded? Yes. Betrayed? Definitely. *How could I have dreamed that? What was wrong with her?* The look on her face as she stared straight ahead told me she wasn't going to say anything else. So I crept back to the room I shared with five other sisters and one brother and stayed in bed, alone, until dinner time.

I remained confused for a long time after that. Mom and I stopped talking altogether. My world had forever changed yet again on the night Mom walked into their bedroom and found me and Daddy in bed. It wasn't my doing and there was no one I could turn to who might explain it to me.

When Mom didn't always have answers to a lot of my questions about things regarding my brothers and sisters, I went to our neighbors. Those with white hair had answers. I remember asking a question of a man who seemed like a mountain to me, almost as wide as he was tall. I don't remember the question, but I do remember him responding in a gentle, resonating tone, "Don't you think that's an adult question?"

"Well, don't you think it deserves an adult answer?" I retorted, stamping my feet with hands on my small hips.

The neighbors were always eager to answer questions after my encounter with the mountain. But I didn't go to them with my shame. I didn't know what I had done. But I didn't want them to think I was a bad person so I didn't talk to any one. I couldn't say anything to the few friends I had. Somehow, they seemed to change. They weren't the same as before so I withdrew from them. Concentrating more and more on home, I did whatever I could to get back in my parents good graces.

Mom had shared the story of how on the eve of each of her parents deaths, she had seen a bright light, like a spotlight, suspended over the spot where they were to be buried. I wanted her to know we shared something in common when, several weeks later, playing by myself on the living room floor, I saw a picture in my head that was similar to watching a television screen. I looked up at Mom and matter-of-factly stated, "Daddy's dead."

Mom stopped midway in lighting the cigarette dangling from her mouth. Tilting her head to one side and with one eyebrow slightly raised, she stared at me silently then slowly lit her cigarette. Turning her back, she walked into the kitchen.

Hours later, two policemen came to the door and said Daddy had died in a car accident. They spoke in low voices but I had heard one of them whisper the word alcohol. There were times after that when Mom would just sit and stare at me. I never knew what she was thinking, and her silence scared me. She had changed so much. We all had. Where there was once a family, a group of strangers now lived in our house.

A few months later we moved from the government housing

into a three-bedroom house in a suburb. Soon after, Mom gave birth to her eighth child, a second boy. Throwing myself into the task of taking care of my newest brother, at eight years of age, I also took on the role of surrogate mother to my other six siblings.

Cinquefoil—Beloved child

Efficiency became my ultimate goal: getting the kids (my children now) ready for school; and helping with their homework; working at home after school. I did anything to fill in the hours of the day.

Our new basement smelled dank and musty with its thick cement walls. My uncle told me boogey men lived there. Imagining them, I didn't go down the stairs unless I ran down them really fast. Boogeymen could trip you by putting their hands through the open steps—according to my nine-year-old brain.

Other unaccustomed fears crept into my soul as I nurtured seeds of insecurity, planted ever so gently in my mind. I heard things in the night, always on alert. I had never before been afraid of the dark. But now the inky darkness became my enemy with all kinds of monsters lurking in the shadows, waiting to pounce on me. I looked into corners and crevices inside dark rooms to see if anything or anyone crouched there, to catch me off guard. Even in the daytime, my bedroom, my closet, and under my bed, didn't escape my scrutiny.

My brother teased me unmercifully on the way to school. He ran ahead of me several blocks then hid behind a tree. When I got to the tree, he jumped out and hollered "Boo." When I peed myself, I became angry. One day, after learning to check out the differences in the street corners and the houses, I ran ahead of *him*. Thinking I was just fooling around, he didn't bother to chase me. I saw panic on his face, though, when he finally arrived at school. I stood behind the cover of the school door, waiting. When I saw him half-running up the walk, I turned my back and walked to my classroom.

Needing to escape, I began walking farther away from our house. I visited the elderly neighbors next door on the corner; those across the street on the corner, and sometimes with the girls across the street. Feeling adventurous one day, I walked to the end of our long block. Now feeling bold, I took a few more steps toward the next corner, a shorter block, before glancing back toward my house. *It doesn't seem such a long way home.* Spotting a few colorful flowers in the backyard of the house on that other corner, I stood on tiptoes and craned my neck to better see. *I smell cookies.* I dared a few more nervous steps forward until a small part of the backyard came into view. *There are a lot of flowers!*

Intrigued, I thought of *our* backyard and its rock-hard dirt from eight kids playing in it so much. Retracing my few steps to the corner, I looked beyond five houses to the sanctuary of our dirt front yard. *If I don't cross any streets, retracing my way back home will be a cinch.* I thought I heard laughter coming from the house of flowers.

My curiosity piqued, I pushed aside my fears as I tiptoed closer. When I got to the bushes surrounding the house, next to the side-walk, I held my breath as I peered over the neatly trimmed hedge. When I saw her, I crept farther along the hedge.

I gasped. *She looks like a fairy talking to her flowers.* I squeezed my eyes shut for a few short moments before opening them for another look. Sure enough, the little woman was still there. *Why she's as small as me!* She had a pretty face and snow-white hair gathered into a bun that sat like a topknot on her head. Damp aromas tickled my nose. *It smells a little like our basement.* There were more flowers than I had ever seen in one place. *Crayola doesn't make this many colors.* There was nothing neat in the design of the garden where rusty buckets held tiny rose bushes, daisy-like flowers peppered throughout the garden, and a large leather shoe overflowed with rosettes of hens and chicks. *Aunt Helen has those.* They stuck out of the top and peeked out the side of the tongue. A small path of steppingstones meandered around beds in various stages of preparation, indicating the garden was created one plot at a time and at the whim of its fairy-like owner.

Enchanted, I chuckled when I spotted statues of miniature frogs, rabbits, and squirrels with silly expressions on their faces hidden under bushes and behind strange tree stumps with ivy growing out of their centers. *They look like they want to play.* My eyes found two birdbaths. One was hidden among the tall daisies and the other among delphiniums. One rose bush stood alone, encircled by a foot-high white picket fence. *I wonder why it's all by itself.*

"Hello," the little woman said in a young, smiling voice.

Her voice hit the back of my knees, and I dropped to the ground like a lump of Jell-O. Engrossed in the garden, I had been unaware that the white-haired woman had moved and was now standing on the opposite side of the hedge. *Please, don't let her be mad at me.*

Peering over at me on the ground, she asked, "Young one, why don't you come through the gate and meet us?"

Embarrassed at having been caught spying, my movements were slow and awkward. *Boy is Mom going to tan my hide.* It took a few moments for my heart to slowly settle back into my chest. *Did she say 'us?' There's no one else in there.* I wanted to run, but her outstretched hand beckoned me. *She's so pretty.* Creating a memory for when I would be alone, I held the vision of her baby-like face with no wrinkles. The sunlight created a soft halo around her head, highlighting little wisps of tiny curls. I couldn't tell if her eyes were soft blue, hazel, or gray.

"Come on," she chirped as she extended her hand over the hedge. On weak legs I allowed her to guide me to the gate. *Her hands are as small as mine and feel like fine sand paper.*

With sweaty, dirty palms and butterflies in my stomach, I stepped through the gate as she held it open for me. *She smells good.* Touching her hand again was like touching joy because it washed away all my fears. Only then did I realize that I hadn't felt good in a long time.

We walked slowly through her yard, gently touching the flowers. *I wish Mom had money for flowers.* I was walking in a dreamland from which I never wanted to awaken as I listened to her mellow voice and her soft-stepping feet. Somewhere within me an ember in the dead ashes of my soul rekindled and started to glow.

Smiling, she named each flower and told me its history, both of us knowing I probably wouldn't remember them. Inhaling the rich scent of flowers and damp earth exhilarated me; feeling the coolness of concrete paving stones and bumpy wood mulch under my dirty, bare feet calmed me. I knelt down to peer eye-to-eye with the concrete critters. *They do want to play.*

Touching some of the flowers in the little woman's garden evoked images of the satin I wasn't allowed to touch when we shopped for sturdy cotton fabric for school clothes. While strolling, she taught me awareness of the lines in, and the velvet softness of the petals of the roses, the fine hair on the leaves of other plants, and the stiff vein supporting each leaf. I wanted desperately for time to stand still as I immersed myself in a world where it was just me, my teacher, and her undivided attention. I loved the little woman's patient voice and her small lips, always smiling. I had never before met an angel. *I wonder why I want to cry.* I reached up and smeared away a tear.

A lot of her teaching was done with gestures as well as spoken words because somehow she knew I couldn't hear well. I was forced to look at people's lips to make out what they were saying. I could hear sounds, but couldn't always make out the words. Two years later, the Lions organization would pay for Mastoid surgery on my right ear.

By the time we got to her house, she gestured a drinking motion. I smelled a sweet, spicy aroma wafting through her screen door. *I hope she offers a cookie.* Smiling, I stepped up into her small kitchen. It welcomed me with its tiny table with a red-and-white checked tablecloth and black-and-white tiles on the floor. I looked at the white counters, the short, squared icebox, and the small four-burner gas stove. *I wonder if this is how all little people live.*

Slowly, I turned in a circle with one hand clasped over the other *(Don't touch that, young lady!)*, until I spied a small cupboard containing dishes almost as small as play dishes. They were ornately painted with tiny red and pink flowers and gold-trimmed edges. There were cups with their saucers, slightly larger plates standing on edge behind them, a matching teapot, and even a lace doily spilled over the shelf displaying its crocheted edge.

Seeing where I was looking, she took a plate off the shelf and handed it to me. I could see her hand through the plate in the sunlight from the door and shook my head. *Mom would tan my hide for sure if I dropped that.* All the while she explained how she had bought the dishes in England when she and her husband had taken a trip there one summer.

"Where's he now?" I asked, looking around, expecting him to peek around a corner from the other room

"He passed away a few years ago." Her chest heaved in a sigh before she briskly asked with a sudden smile, "Do you want some cookies and milk now?" *This I can do.* She took down a plate from the white cupboard. While she poured the milk, I scooted up onto a wooden, straight-backed chair and stared at the blue-and-white checked napkin she had placed in my lap. *What am I supposed to do with this?* No one had ever given me a napkin before. I became self-conscious of my worn dress and dirty hands and fingernails.

With the large cookie in my hand, I glanced at her, then down at the napkin again and then back to her. She chuckled softly before explaining what to do with the thing in my lap. *She makes me feel so special.* My cheeks ached from smiling so much, but I didn't care. I had found a special friend.

Visiting every chance I could as the spring and summer weeks passed, I enjoyed many such tea parties. She chattered about everything and nothing and I listened with starving ears. Feeling grown-up, I imagined myself having such tea parties with my own little girl. For certain, if I'd had dolls, I would have made them pretty dresses and had imaginary tea parties with them. The little woman and I traveled to exotic places through her stories: I felt the coldness of Alaska; smelled the salt water on an ocean cruise; and climbed the green hills of Ireland. The question of whether or not she had actually traveled to those places didn't matter. I only knew that my imagination ran high as she helped me to escape from my dysfunctional world and swept me far away from my corner of the block.

One day I saw Mom leave the little woman's house and go in the opposite direction and I was scared. I hid behind the bushes until she was out of sight. *No, Mom. She's mine. I don't want to share her.* The little woman was my special angel. I knew I was being selfish in keeping her to myself, but I just couldn't talk to anyone about her. I was afraid if I did, I wouldn't be able to visit her or she would just disappear. Neither Mom nor the little woman ever said anything, nor did I see Mom at the house of flowers again.

Spending as much time as I could with her and her garden, I learned how to touch the flowers more than I learned how to care for them. Unwittingly, I learned to touch with consciousness, to listen, not only to the sounds of the wind and the birds, but to the silence as well. I learned to discern and separate scents and fragrances in my head as they passed through my nose. The little woman embraced me often. Her hugs were deliberate, firm, yet gentle. She loved me by smiling at me when she handed me my hot chocolate, by listening intently with occasional pointed questions when I related stories of my family. Always, there was a warm fuzzy feeling whenever she was near.

Finding her asleep on the couch one day nearly scared me out of my mind. I shook her hard. "Lord, child, you'll push me through the couch," she said, smiling until she saw the expression on my face. "Honey, I'm fine. I was just tired."

"I was scared. You aren't supposed to get sick," I said in a shaky voice and saw my hands trembling. My fear seemed unreasonable and, for the first time in my life, I found myself relying upon someone as one would rely upon an immovable rock.

The little woman rose from the sofa, explaining, "Ed, my neighbor next door, hasn't been feeling well, and I've been keeping an eye on him until his family gets here."

"Is he all right?" I asked, placing my hand on her floral apron. We were at the kitchen sink where she ran water into her teakettle for tea and hot chocolate. We talked like two people having a conversation, not like one behaving as a child and the other an adult. I knew I could ask the little woman anything.

"That's making you sick too. I don't want you sick. I wouldn't know how to take care of you," I stated flatly, wiping away a tear.

She stopped setting the table and looked at me. "Young one, my friend needs God's hands, and I intend to give them to him."

Sitting in my chair, I stopped eating my cookie and stared at her. *Sometimes that woman can say the most outlandish things.* "How can you give him God's hands when they are attached to God?" I shook my head. *She can be so silly.* My voice must have sounded incredulous because she dropped down into her chair, placed her hands in her lap, and silently studied me. I felt she saw right through to my soul, examining my brain, looking at every one of my cells.

The whistling teakettle shattered the silence.

Getting up, the little woman slowly brought the teakettle to the table, looking like she was throwing all manner of things around in her head. She remained silent as she poured the water into my cup and into her teapot with the teabag in it. She then placed the teapot on the trivet, covered it with a tea cozy and put the pot of hot water on the stove. Coming back to the table, she absentmindedly stirred my hot chocolate. *Does she think I can't stir it any more?* I stared at her, wondering if she was okay.

After a few more moments she sat down in her chair and peered at me before asking, "What do you know of God?"

I stopped swinging my legs and put down my cookie. It was my turn to put my hands in my lap. I knew by her tone of voice and the deep silence that this was important. Even the clock in the living room seemed to stop ticking, as if it, too, waited for my answer.

"I know that God loves me and that if I don't behave He will punish me," and then quickly added, "if the devil doesn't get me first." I sat silently for a moment. "You know, with both of them after me, I used to be afraid to do anything." Leaning forward I whispered in a conspiratorial voice, "And sometimes I do things just to see what they will do. And you know what? Nothing happens." I leaned back in my chair, quite pleased with myself.

She smiled and said, "That's because God wishes us to be well and happy. He doesn't want to hurt us nor wish us harm." There was a pause before she spoke again. "Folks say that in the beginning there was a big bang, and the universe grew from that, expanding every day. Out of the big bang came all the little sparks of God, and these sparks, too, grow and expand every day."

In my nine-year-old mind I had a picture of this huge man pointing a gun at the sky and pulling the trigger. Puzzled, I said, "I don't understand. Why would God shoot a gun?"

Chuckling, she responded, "Actually, it was a big explosion of sorts. It's a little difficult to explain because we don't have the words to describe it. Know this: Everything existing in this whole, wide universe," she made a broad outward sweep of her arms, "is God. He's everything, everywhere, at all times."

I looked at my half-eaten cookie, my eyes widening in fear. "Did I just eat God?"

Softly laughing, she said, "Yes, I guess you did." I was on the verge of crying when she bent over to hug me "Honey, its okay. Let me explain it another way. God made everything that exists. Can you understand that?"

"Uh-huh," I responded, nodding my head before looking at my good-tasting cookie. *God is a good cook.*

"He even made our souls, which can also be called the spark of God, or the light of God." She thought for a moment before continuing. "Because everything came from God, you could say all things are tiny Gods. We can't do everything God does because we are only a tiny part of Him. But if you put everything in the universe together, you have God. Can you see this?" she gently asked.

I related to her my picture of this man made of light exploding into tiny sparks. She raised her hands over her head and laughed out loud before saying, "We'll go with that for now."

Her laughter permeated the kitchen, and I couldn't help but laugh, too, until I remembered. "Aren't you going to tell me about God's hands?"

"Our souls are the light of God, or the spark of God. Are you with me?" she asked.

"Yep." I was getting into it now.

"Since we are a small spark of a big God, are we not small Gods?" she asked, leaning her head to one side.

Now here was a grown-up question, and I was going to give it the attention it deserved. I screwed up my face to look as though I was giving things a long, hard think; but the truth of the matter was, it made perfect sense to me. I put the cookie down as I wondered aloud about miracles God made.

She's so pretty when she smiles. "We can create small miracles, young one. When someone is sick, we can help him or her with their housework, or hold their hand. We can plant flowers for their beauty." Her back yard came to mind. "We can watch birds as they hatch out of their eggs, or babies being born. Why, young one, there's even a little miracle in hugging someone who is sad. God creates so many little miracles every day that we'd be hard-pressed to see all of them. Truth be known, so many people are looking for that big miracle, they miss the little ones."

When she hugged me, I understood what she was saying about the miracle of a hug. I always felt the movement of warmth all the way down to the bottoms of my feet when she or Granny, my Mom's aunt, embraced me.

Our conversation that afternoon never left me. I carried it in my heart whenever I passed even a dandelion: I remembered it when my baby sister was crying, and marveled at the little miracle when my hug stopped her tears.

I floated for several days, all the while creating every miracle I could. Sometimes I was impatient in getting people's permission. The little woman said to always get people's permission before doing anything for them. It was hard because I wanted so badly to create a little miracle every single day, every hour. It felt so good to feel good.

About a week later, I went to the flower garden and heard my little woman crying at the kitchen table. Worried, I slowly approached her because I didn't want to frighten her. She hadn't heard me, so I did the only thing I knew to do. I gave her the only miracle I had—I hugged her. She patted my hand, but kept crying. I had no idea what was wrong, but my chest ached at the sounds of her tears.

Helplessness made me desperate. Not wanting to invade her space, I slowly tiptoed outside. I needed a bigger miracle.

Looking around the garden, I spotted her favorite rose bush in its fenced bed and caught sight of the most perfect bud. It was her favorite rose in her favorite color, and it was in bud; but the garden shears were in the house and I wanted to surprise her. Trying to snap off the bud as I had seen her do, I succeeded only in bending the stem. Tugging at it didn't work, and pulling harder, my hand slipped up the stem. Tears of frustration flowed down my face before it suddenly occurred to me to bite the stem with my teeth, the way I cut sewing thread. It tasted bitter and took a lot of chewing before the bud finally came lose in my hand. Triumphantly, I ran toward the house. Never mind the bottom of the stem was bent and badly shredded. Blood smeared on the rose petal didn't look too good either. I walked to the back door and saw the little woman sitting up in the chair blowing her nose into a handkerchief. Cautiously, I walked up to her and handed her the rose.

She froze. Her face blanched at the sight of my hands. Without saying a word she shot out of her chair and went to the kitchen cupboard where she grabbed the peroxide, brought down a bowl, and ran hot water into it. She then went into the bathroom and came out with a washcloth, towel, and cotton balls.

Not one word was said. *She's angry with me.* She sat on her kitchen stool and placed my hands in her lap. She began washing my hands with a gentleness that scared me. They were starting to hurt by then and I understood why when I glanced down at them. I had several lacerations from thorns, one of which was still in my palm.

Taking out the thorn she touched the spot with a cotton ball soaked with peroxide then sat and stared at me. When I looked into her face I saw fresh tears falling onto her cheeks.

I felt so bad. Looking at the water I said, "I'm sorry about the rose, but I didn't want you to be sad. It hurt me to see you crying, and my hug didn't do anything." I put my head in her lap. I had never been stroked before. *Please, let me stay here.*

Lifting my head with her fingers and looking me in the eye, she said, "Child, I was sad because my friend next door passed away last night." She paused only for a moment to run a finger along my cheek, smiling as she inhaled a deep breath before continuing. "I just never thought that before I died I would be wiping blood off the hands of God."

No one had ever considered me good enough to be a spark of God. It was my turn to cry.

*

A few Saturdays later I walked into her kitchen to find the table formally set in a formal array. Her fancy cups and teapot were on the table with a small platter full of cookies, and a vase held a rose from her garden. Linen napkins were nestled beside smaller plates. Surprised, I turned to leave. The little woman hadn't said a word about expecting company.

"Where are you going?" she queried with a cheery voice, raising her eyebrows.

"You've got company coming." I pointed to the table.

"She's here." And, with a formal air, she took my hand and walked me the few short steps to my chair and seated me. I became nervous when she pushed my chair closer to the table for me.

"You're my very special friend, and I thought it time we had a special tea." She sat down across from me. "What's the matter, honey?"

"I don't know what to do?" I wanted very much to please her, but I felt out of place. *This doesn't feel good. Something's not right.*

"A friend of mine a long time ago showed me how the high society girls behaved. If you want I can show you." She didn't wait for a reply. "Your napkin goes on your lap, like so." She took her napkin off the table, gave it a little shake and placed it on her lap. "Now, you try it."

I took the white linen napkin, saw the dirt under my fingernails and hid my hands in my lap. She grabbed my hand. "Its okay, honey. We're not going to worry about that,"Then she poured the hot liquid into my prepared cup. Elated, I gulped the hot, sweet liquid. *It's real tea!*

For two hours we giggled over her stories and laughed at poking out our pinkies when we sipped our tea. No shoes, grimy feet, worn dress, unkempt hair, dirty fingernails, and I felt like a high society girl sitting up straight, head held high, a napkin in my lap, my pinky out, and properly nibbling at my cookie. The little woman even showed me how to dissolve sugar in my teacup without clanking the sides with my spoon. Oh, how that impressed me. She asked me about school and I spent the afternoon telling her secrets I had never before told anyone.

Because I helped with canning, and school was starting, two weeks passed before I was able to visit the little woman again. I ran up behind her at the rose bush, reached around her waist and gave her my usual hug. Only when she turned around did I see it wasn't the little woman. I was shocked more than she. I looked toward the kitchen door. "She's not here," the stranger said with a sad smile.

Puzzled and nervous, I asked, "Why not?" My heart raced, its pulse pounding in my head.

"You're Lady, aren't you?" She brightened at the discovery. "Alice told me so much about you."

"Alice?" I gasped. *I never knew her name.* It never seemed important to know or use each other's name.

"Yes, dear. My name is Marianne, and Alice was my sister."

Staring at her, I stood there while my chest tightened. I wished it was late spring, and I was barefoot, walking into the garden for the first time. I thought of traveling to London, India… Seeing my confusion, Marianne softly stated, "Honey, Alice passed away early yesterday evening." Patiently, she waited.

"Alice lived here?" I asked, pointing to the ground. It still felt strange to hear and say her name, as though we were talking about someone else. I was praying it *was* someone else.

"Are you okay?"

I nodded, my body responding on its own. Not knowing what else to do, I turned to leave.

"Lady, I have something for you." She went into the kitchen

and came out with a box. "It's the tea service Alice loved so much." And she placed it in my hands.

In my mind's eye, I saw the little woman laughing during the last tea party we had, with the pretty dishes, while images of what she had taught me danced across my vision. I even felt her loving embraces. Thinking back over the months, no matter what I did or said, I was never criticized or scolded, but was shown the appropriate way to do or say a thing. I realized then how very important she was to me and how much I had loved her, still loved her. *I never told her I loved her.* Tears streamed down my cheeks.

Looking down at the box in my arms, I knew my brothers and sisters would break the beautiful tea set that came from across the ocean so many years ago. That would be like seeing the little woman broken; the one who thought my hands were the hands of God.

I lifted the box to Marianne and said, "Thank you, but I don't want it."

Turning, I left her standing there, her mouth gaping. My hand upon the gate, I closed it with a soft click as I walked out of the garden—without looking back.

Nasturtium—Resignation

Devastated by the loss of my little woman, I found school that fall and winter especially hard; and there was no one with whom to share my grief. I missed her company, her softness, her voice, everything about her, especially her stories about exotic places. They had helped me to escape the burden of my environment. I felt like my heart had been cut out when she died and, I needed to get a piece of it back just to feel it beating again.

In the spring, I went back to the little woman's house. Walking the long way around the block and approaching from opposite direction than I had when I first went there. I slowed as I neared her house. Something was different. I stopped and looked into the yard, now bare of a hedge on the other side of the house. Nor was there a gate, or any signs of a gate. I looked around me. *Have I gone around the wrong block?* Thinking that perhaps the yard might look more familiar from the side where I would have entered the garden, I slowly walked around the corner.

Where the special rose bush had stood was a child's swing, looking as though it had rusted into place for years, untouched. Small patches of mud gleamed where the large paving stones used to be. All the flowers were gone, along with the beds. No critters smiled anywhere. There was nothing from before except the house. Even it looked seedy and rundown. Paint was chipping off the windows, and the back door was dirty with a torn screen. The shock was too much for my ten-year-old brain as I stood there by the scene. *Had she even existed? She had to! I should have taken the tea set as proof. Where did everything go?*

My heart tripped when I heard a woman's throaty voice from the doorway. "Can I help you?"

It was enough to jerk me back into reality. "No. No, thank you." I turned away. Continuing around the block, I shrugged my shoulders and straightened my back. In the time it took me to walk back home, I started to push the little woman out of my head. *I had a wonderful summer last year, living in my imagination.*

Things come hard. They go easy.

✻

As the younger ones got older, they took over some of the smaller chores. Gaining a new sense of freedom at the age of ten, I began roaming the neighborhood and found some boys a block away. I stopped wearing dresses and became a tomboy in blue jeans. Boys didn't have to stay home and work as hard as girls did and had more fun. I didn't want to be a girl, because girls birthed babies, and there had been days when all I did was babysit and work with Mom.

That summer I escaped every chance I got. If I wasn't running, I was bicycling, climbing trees, always showing off—always moving, never still, and always thinking of mischief. I did nothing that would harm anyone, but did anything that brought me attention. I accepted every dare the boys issued. I out-wrestled, out-climbed, and out-ran them. But they were faster on a bicycle. That was all right, though. I wrestled them to the ground when we stopped, and before long I won the bike races too.

Mom brought a man home who stayed with us periodically. The relationship didn't last long, though. We kids liked him because he made us laugh. So I didn't think too much about it when my future second stepfather came on the scene. We had no idea where he came from, except that Mom met him at work. She still had the same job at the bar/restaurant. I usually smelled alcohol on his breath and became uneasy around him. I was especially concerned when he treated me extra nice. Mom noticed too. It didn't stop her from marrying him, though

Mom birthed my third brother six months after she married my new step-father. I wasn't angry about the house being full of nine kids. I just kept up with the new chores as best I could. I devised new ways of escaping the house, and when I couldn't escape, I ate. One day, tired of the house, the kids, everything, I tried to go out and play but Mom stopped me. That made me angry. She was married now so there should have been some letup; instead, there were more chores.

A shouting match ensued. I finally hollered, tears brimming my eyes, "Why can't I go out?"

A combination of hate and sadness crossed Mom's face. In a soft voice, she responded, "Because you're all I've got."

I said nothing, but I went to the door and told the guys I couldn't come out.

She never had to say that to me again.

Daisy—Innocence

Granny made one of her rare visits when I was eleven. She was Mom's aunt, but everyone called her Granny. Being innovative when we kids acted up and she wanted us to be quiet, Mom would ask Granny to brush her hair. Fascinated, we sat quietly and stared while Granny slowly removed the three hair pins from her bun, allowing her hair to fall gracefully down to her ankles. She was only five feet tall but it was still a lot of hair to us. Taking up her hair brush, she started at the top of her head and slowly pulled it through her hair to the ends, while lifting her hair until all of it ended up on her lap. It took a full minute for each stroke, and each stroke hypnotized us into total silence. It wasn't until after I was married and taking care of other children that I realized how clever Mom had been. It was during those times we were quiet and occupied that she could get things done for herself.

Granny, with her warm embraces, was like the little woman, and I was always the lucky one to share a bed with her when she stayed with us. She told me she liked hugs, and it was okay to hug her while we slept together. Those were the only times I was hugged. At this point in my life, Granny was the only person I trusted. She had never lied to me and never treated me like a child.

We were in the basement talking quietly while doing the laundry. It had been four years since Daddy had hurt me and the 'nightmare' stayed with me. I still dreamed of seeing Mom with the gun and remembered what she had said. When the washer and the two tubs had drained and Granny and I were wiping them out, it occurred to me to ask her the question burning in my mind those four long, troubling years.

"Granny, can I ask you something?" I held my breath.

"Yes, child." She looked at me with a soft smile curving her mouth. She always smelled of the rich, pleasant mixture of snuff and peppermint.

I related to her what had happened that night when Mom had found me with Daddy.

Lowering her eyes, it was a few moments before she raised her head. "Have you talked with your mother about this?"

Silence stilled my heart for half a beat before resonating off the walls and around the room, surrounding us.

"Yes. But she tells me it was a nightmare." Then I forced out, "And I know it wasn't, Granny," and I started crying. Mom's rejection was still an open wound in my heart. It also hurt because she hadn't trusted me with the truth.

The bare light bulb over our heads cast a dingy yellow glow. A shaft of sunlight coming in through the small, square basement window highlighted dancing dust motes in the thick air, full of the damp, earthy odors of the basement. The smell of bleach still clung as the sound of water dripping into the floor drain intensified in the silence. My heart pulsed in my throat, drying it out. I would dissolve in that pool of water in which I stood if Granny, too, told me that it was a nightmare. I could not bear it if she, too, had turned on me.

She looked at me, and I saw tears well up in her eyes and fall on her cheeks as she whispered, "Child, I cannot speak to you of this." She then gave me a hug that felt different from any I had ever received from her before. Turning around, she walked through the other room and up the stairs, her soft footsteps echoing in the thick silence.

Each drop dripping into the drain sounded like a small explosion to my ears. As my heart beat fell into rhythm with each drop, my trust in my family drained away. With each beat of my heart, my trust in love flowed out into the city sewer. In those moments, loud with silence, I realized three things: I wasn't crazy after all because I now knew I hadn't dreamed the nightmare; I would never lie to another no matter how much the truth might hurt; and since I wasn't able to rely on anyone, I would always stand alone.

Granny had not lied to me, but I understood our not speaking of such things because speaking of them would make them so real as to be intolerable. That was the way it was with my family and its Southern roots. Little stupid, lies were always told. I never understood this habit when everyone knew the lie could and would be so easily proven.

In the days that followed memories flashed through my head.

The year before, having watched Ed Sullivan on TV, I was in the backyard with my siblings dancing, singing, and doing whatever else I thought we could do to put on a neighborhood show for which we could charge people a penny. I had even engaged the girls across the street to act in a skit I had written. When I mentioned my plans to Dad, he responded, "Who's going to be stupid enough to pay a penny to watch a bunch o' kids?" Crestfallen and feeling foolish, I dropped the show and stopped doing anything creative with my sisters and brothers.

I also remembered stepping into the large Salvation Army truck that had come around giving out toys to *needy* children for Christmas. When I pointed to a paint set when I was offered a doll, the man told me in a hateful voice, "Young lady you should be thankful to God for whatever you get and not be choosy." When he shoved the paint set at me, I handed it back to him. Standing as tall as I could, I responded, "Please give this to someone who needs it." I walked off the truck and never entered it again. I stopped doing anything artistically at home.

Ticking off each memory one by one as they flashed by on my mental screen, I saw the futility of getting approval or attention from my parents. Mom was too busy with working, the kids, and the house. And Dad was too much into his alcohol. I stopped trying to gain my parents' love and approval and again looked to the elderly people of the neighborhood.

Having lost both parents before she was fourteen and gave birth to me before she was sixteen, my mother was shunned by society. She learned to not bring attention upon herself, not to ask questions, and to do the best she could. I couldn't buy that. It hadn't taken me long the first time to learn that those in the neighborhood with gray hair not only had answers but had the time and patience to teach me.

There were three elderly women within one or two houses of us, and I visited them often. They weren't the little woman, but they never made me feel stupid or awkward, either. They taught me to take care of my brothers and sisters and at the same time taught me how to take care of myself: "It's okay to do for others but if you don't take care of yourself and get sick, you won't be able to take care of anyone else." That scared me. I knew no one could take care of my brothers and sisters the way I did. Those women understood and said nothing when either Mom or I went to visit them. Actually, Mom and I weren't aware of the other's visit to the older women for advice. They offered both of us individual times of respite: Mom, when it was her turn, coffee; and me, when it was my turn, a cola or water. We never went together—someone had to stay home to watch the kids.

✻

Rosebud–Youth

Six small grocery stores operated within a few blocks of our house. Though Mom shopped weekly at the large grocery store in the mall, I frequented the smaller ones when we ran out of things. Tony's Grocery filled the narrow first floor of a house. By the time I was eleven, I was an experienced shopper and errand runner. Also by this time my body had filled out, and I was made aware of this during one of my visits.

I walked to the back of the store and spotted Tony behind the meat counter using his cleaver on a large carcass on the huge two-foot-thick butcher block. When I asked for the hamburger, he motioned for me to come back behind the counter. I felt special as I walked around the glass. He asked me if I wanted to see his meat. Confused, and glancing at the butcher block, I nodded. He took my hand and led me into the walk-in cooler.

Once we were behind the steel door, he immediately spun me around so that my back was against his bloody apron. Putting his smelly hands on my breasts, he began rubbing them in a circular motion. His action was so abrupt and so unexpected, I couldn't think. Shocked and scared, I instinctively pulled away from him and ran to the cooler door, which stood slightly ajar. I shoved it open and raced past the butcher block. Then I remembered the hamburger. I stopped and turned around and there was Tony standing at his block, the meat cleaver in one hand suspended above his head, the other hand holding onto the carcass.

With an ugly sneer, he growled, "If we don't play, your mama is going to get nothing but fat for hamburger."

When the cleaver dropped heavily onto the block, my body moved like a cannon had shot me out the side door. I ran home as fast as my legs would move. I bolted through the kitchen door.

Startled, Mom turned from the stove and demanded, "What's wrong?"

Gasping, I told her what Tony had done and said. Staring at me, her face took on an angry expression. In another moment Mom went through the swinging, two-way kitchen door into the dining room and came back with her purse. Handing me another dollar, she ordered through tight, hard lips, "Go to the store on Seventh."

God, am I supposed to go to another store and have that owner feel my breasts? I threw the dollar back at her, spun around, and stomped out the back kitchen door.

Mom should have gone back to Tony's and told him off, slapped him hard in the face. Hamburger for supper was more important than I was, even if it was going to cost a dear dollar more. I didn't know where I was going, but it had to be away from home. I wanted to run away, as far away as I could. But there was no place to go. The guys had begun doing their thing with their 'no girls allowed' club. The girls across the street were on their annual family camping trip. There was no one to whom I could turn. I couldn't go to the older people because I was so ashamed, of myself, and of Mom.

It was several hours before I came home and everyone was sitting at the supper table when I walked in. I tried to walk past them on my way to my room, but Mom called my name and pointed to my chair. Like a good girl, I shuffled to the table and sat down. My eyes watered the whole time I shoved the spaghetti around on my plate. Mom was the only one who noticed I didn't eat.

By the fall of seventh grade, I had changed from a smiling outgoing girl into a quiet, morose child who felt like a nonentity. I started walking the two and half miles to middle school with the two older girls from across the street. On the days they took the school bus, I walked alone. Even in the rain, I walked a half mile to a small store during my lunch hour then back to school with a candy bar or something. When the snow fell, I enjoyed listening to the whisper of cars' tires as they moved over the packed snow. The earth stilled as the hush of winter gradually enveloped it; and there were times I wished it would envelop me as well, bury me deep.

During my lone walks, I reflected on my experiences with the male population, and wondered what had attracted them, still considering myself an ugly duckling. I thought about my brothers and sisters and what would happen to them when I left home, because I was hell-bent on leaving at eighteen. The time after that stretched into what I began to look upon as a void. There were no fears, since I had walked daily in a void since the little woman had died.

Lonely, I explored the streets the following spring, expanding my territory every time I ventured out. There was always this thing, a sense of urgency inside me, an *it*. If I kept moving, *it* stayed behind me. If I stopped, I feared *it* would catch up and we'd meet. That never really made sense to me. What I did understand was that I was angry inside all the time.

One spring day I met a girl who had enormous breasts. I mean, they were all I saw when she approached me, and she wasn't hiding them. In fact, the way she walked and carried herself, I knew she was deliberately accentuating her chest. I stayed with her a little while that day. Jennie was a couple of years older than I, but it didn't matter when we learned how much we had in common. We used to strike dramatic poses as we lip-synced to Ricky Nelson or Elvis Presley, and took turns dressing up and discovering we liked the same clothes and colors. We laughed a lot that first day together. It surprised me to discover how little I laughed and how awkward I sounded.

She taught me about clothes and fashion. We shopped after school and I put things on layaway with my babysitting money. Mom suggested I save my money, but it made me feel good to spend it, a great sense of satisfaction. I embraced myself with new and different things as often as I could.

Toward the end of my seventh grade, my English teacher, tall, square-built and very unassuming, asked me to join him out in the hall. I didn't know what to expect. I waited while he looked at the wall behind me for a few moments before looking down at me. Clearing his throat, he said, "Lady, you're not doing well in English, and I feel that, as your teacher, I have failed you somehow. I'm sorry for this. And because I have failed, I'm not going to fail *you*. I'm going to give you a passing grade and hope that your next English teacher will be someone with whom you can relate."

Shock nailed me to the floor. *Is this guy for real?* I knew my grades weren't good: I was having too much fun with Jennie to care. But standing before me was an adult who was apologizing because he thought he had failed me. Everything had always been *my* fault, not someone else's. I couldn't respond to him; I didn't know how to respond. I just stood there and stared at him in disbelief. His gentle nudge on my shoulder unglued my feet from the floor, and we walked back into the classroom. All the other kids turned their heads and stared with curiosity, expecting to see me upset in some way. I walked back to my seat, and, like a young lady, brushed my skirt forward under me and sat down. That was the last time any teacher had reason to talk to me about my grades. Someone had believed in me. Finally, someone cared. I had done something wrong, yet had been forgiven.

When Jennie's natural father made plans to take her down south for two weeks during the summer, her mother called Mom to get permission for me to go along. After learning Jennie's father was paying for everything, she allowed me to go. Compared to our annual family picnic to different parks every summer, the idea of going out of state was like going to the other side of the world. Not sleeping much before the trip, I imagined us visiting all sorts of exotic places. Mom bought me shorts and underwear; and Jennie helped me get a dress in case we met some good-looking guys. I was confident Jennie would show me what to do with a boy.

Jennie and her father enjoyed making the trip exciting for me. And I memorized everything I saw and learned to share with my brothers and sisters. We stayed at her cousins' house in Kentucky, where I experienced homemade feather beds and down comforters; I stayed in motels for the first time; and I went to Renfro Valley and the Grand Ole Opry. Though we dined in all kinds of restaurants, I got hooked on hamburgers, fries, and malts. Jeannie's father tried to buy me everything I admired, but Mom had already cautioned me against it. Nevertheless, it felt good to have a man offer to buy me things and not want to hurt me. It showed me that such men, outside of the old ones in the neighborhood, existed.

Jennie and I met boys, though I didn't think them all that good-looking. I watched her parade in front of them and saw the goofy looks on their faces when they stared at her breasts. I studied her; she swished her hips to and fro, took a few steps then cocked her head to one side and looked back, smiling as though she knew a secret. One night she slipped out after dark, without inviting me, and met one of the boys in the barn. Practicing her walk in the bedroom by myself, my stiff hips resisted the side-to-side sashaying. This only engrained in me even more my female ineptness. *What if I had gotten a boy? What would I have done with him out in the barn? Anywhere, for that matter?*

When school started in the fall, Jennie and I saw each other only during lunch time. To give teens something to do with the rest of their lunch hour, the school allowed us to dance to records played in the gym. She and I would dance together in our tight skirts, showing off and looking very adult-like and sexy. Well, she looked sexy and I tried. During spring break, I was proud to introduce Jennie to my tomboy buddies, who were the same age as she. When they saw her chest, their eyes popped, and I became invisible.

Though still growing, I knew my breasts would never look like Jennie's. But I still wanted very much to be desired. When I got home, I helped with dinner then went upstairs and closed my bedroom door. Listening at the door to be sure no one else was upstairs, I turned my back to the mirror and practiced "the walk" Jennie had shown me, turning my head to look into the mirror and smiling a come-hither smile. A waddling duck had more grace, and on me, the smile resembled a painful grimace. Stumbling against the bed and falling on my face didn't help my ego, either. I felt ugly and awkward and hated everyone for leaving me out of things. Pushing myself off the bed, I walked to the door and yanked it open, letting it bang against the wall, and stomped downstairs to dinner. I ate.

Though a late bloomer compared to some of the other girls, I became aware of my adolescence in gym class that fall when I started my period. I was nearly frightened out of my mind when one day I saw blood on my panties and hollered down to Mom. When she came upstairs, I showed her the blood and exclaimed, "I'm dying."

I was dumbstruck when, without a word, she walked out of the bathroom and came back with a Kotex pad and a weird piece of elastic band with two elastic extensions and hooks on the end. She handed me the Kotex and said flatly, "You're not dying; you're having your period. All women have them." She laid the elastic contraption on the sink.

"What's a period," I asked, confused that a dot at the end of a sentence had anything to do with my dying. "And what's this for?" picking up the elastic.

"A woman bleeds every month so she can have babies." She picked up the elastic and added, "This is to keep the Kotex in place." Dropping it back on the sink, she said "You'll figure it out," and walked out.

I was emotionally confused. I didn't know if I was relieved about not dying; scared that I could have babies (and where did they come from, anyway); or angry because I hadn't been told about something every woman does naturally, which would have saved me a near heart attack.

I never did figure out the elastic thing. I fumbled with it for a while; finally, I shoved it in my dresser drawer, and placed the Kotex on my panties. I spent the next several months getting used to something between my legs that didn't belong there.

Gym class was an enormous hurdle for me. I had to take showers with the other girls, and shyness, inexperience, and ignorance overwhelmed me. I glanced at the other girls in the locker room and almost gawked at the different shapes of bodies. I tried to hide mine behind my locker door, knowing they, too, were looking at me. It impressed me that some of the other girls were actually comfortable with their nakedness.

And I became fascinated with the dot the Gym teacher put in the box next to my name. She put it there every time I wore my

Kotex. I was torn between wishing I could see that dot every day of gym class and wearing the Kotex that always stayed twisted.

In mid-winter the Gym class viewed a film about women and their monthly cycles. Hypnotized, I watched it as though the film was made just for me. I remembered when I was about nine years old, I had found a book in mom's bedroom with pictures of front and side views of a naked woman with a baby inside of her. I was so fascinated that I kept going back to look at it, only to discover I had to hunt for it each and every time. Sometime in the past year, after spending a few days hunting for the book, I had asked Mom where she put it and was told she had burned it.

The film shown in gym class animated the lost book. When the film was over, I asked the girl next to me what a menstrual cycle was, and she said that it was my period. *Again, the dot!* When the gym instructor turned on the lights, I caught her looking at me. As I was leaving the locker room, she called me into her office. After I closed the door, she picked up a book from her desk and silently handed it to me. I saw the words "menstruating" and handed it back to her; I was totally embarrassed. I said that I already knew about all that stuff and nearly ran out of her office.

During the next few months my friendship with Jennie waned, and I saw the boys even less. The group disbanded as Jennie and the boys went into high school, leaving me behind.

*

Oats—The witching soul of music

I was unnerved, seeing all the black leather jackets worn by the James Dean and Fonzie types hanging out around the high school building and the nearby streets. I quickly walked up the front steps, seeking the security of the old three-story building that served nearly 2,000 students. The expansive top step was filled with lolling, smug jocks in sweaters adorned with the high school letters and flirting with girls in tight skirts, sweaters, nylons and flats. This was a grown-up world and I was out of my element. Give me children and old people.

Walking into the Music Room on the first floor, I heard an oriole in the bushes outside the open, eight-foot-tall windows, singing to the music played on the piano. Mr. Jones sat at a grand piano in the middle of the room. I just stood there within the room's vast space…listening. My peripheral vision took in the bleachers climbing one wall; the bright singer in the bushes, filling in between the notes Mr. Jones played; and instruments lined up against the far wall. Fresh air wafted through the windows while I memorized the moment. Mr. Jones banged out the final notes on the piano, rose, and walked toward me. Not a tall man, he had a long, angular face with a short black, Dick Clark hairstyle, peppered with a little gray. He moved with a grace that reminded me of what little classical music I had heard. Smiling as he shook my hand, he welcomed me to his classroom before offering me a chair. A gentle man with a soft voice, his demeanor drew respect.

I asked, "How does someone get into the First and Second Choirs, especially the First Choir?" I had heard that the First Choir traveled in the school bus and had burgundy robes. I staked my hopes and aspirations on that burgundy robe, singing alto.

Gesturing with his outstretched hand, he led me to his grand piano. After singing a chorus of a short childhood song, I knew I had failed the solo miserably and stood before the graceful man with tears welling up in my eyes.

Sitting on his piano bench, he peered at me, and in a kind voice, asked "Can you read music?"

"Not much, sir," I responded, abashed.

He patted my hand resting on the piano before getting up. He walked with me to a soundproof room with an upright piano inside.

In the open doorway, he said, "You can't try out for First Choir until the end of your junior year. Your grades will have to be C or above. You'll also need to know how to read music and sing a solo in front of the choir while playing an instrument." I turned to walk away. Touching my shoulder, he added, "I can teach you the piano while you learn to read the music. Do you have a piano at home?"

Bowing my head, I answered, "No sir, just eight younger brothers and sisters. I guess they make enough noise." *He has such a gentle smile.*

"I can write a slip for you to get out of study hall and you can come in here to practice for a little while before and after school."

I thanked him profusely and was so giddy and excited that I forgot the note and my books as I ran out the door and on to my next class. Feeling foolish, I excused myself, explaining I had left my books in the Music Room. The Music Room was empty by then. Spotting my things on a nearby desk, my heart soared to see the note I needed to excuse me from study hall. Another note, to me, stated that Mr. Jones expected me to be there thirty minutes early before school and to stay thirty minutes after school! As I walked home after school, it occurred to me that I hadn't told him my class schedule, and so I decided he was a magician as well a musician. Sleep eluded me that night.

I spent the next few months getting used to new routines at school and at home. Going to bed late became the norm as homework and practicing shorthand took up my evenings. Gregg shorthand was a written language at which I excelled. On rare occasions the teacher chose me to go up in front of the class to dictate letters at 150 words per minute. I've talked fast since I was five. When you get cut off often enough, you learn to get your words out. I loved shorthand and practiced for hours at night, getting lost in shaping the new letters, forming precise words and making sure they were the same size as those in the textbook, neat and concise. Shorthand became my friend; we understood each other.

Freshmen were sometimes teased, but, for the most part, we were just ignored. I learned right away who the male jocks were by their struts. Female jocks were snobbish and always huddled in groups, giggling and holding their books tight to their chests, until a male jock happened to pass by. Now there was a scenario to watch from behind my hall locker door. Janie sees Johnny strutting toward her, so she drops her book right in front of him. "Hey, Janie, you dropped your book," Johnny would say and make a big show of handing it to dewy-eyed Janie. You'd have thought the book had fallen over a cliff and it had been life-threatening to retrieve it.

"Why thank you, Johnny. You look really nice in your school jacket," she would respond with a sappy smile while batting her eyes—like he'd gone over that cliff just for her. *If she wanted him so badly, why couldn't she just walk up to him and say so?* It seemed like a lot of fuss for a whole lot of nothing.

Ninth grade flew by for a fifteen year old with a schedule filled with Mr. Jones for thirty minutes in the morning and afternoon, studying, and helping out at home. There wasn't time to worry about being popular. I occasionally walked to school with the two girls across the street, they having joined their older sister in high school. But, I mainly walked alone, having discovered that I was too old for most girls my age; they were so frivolous and too young for me. I had stopped asking Mom and Dad questions because we didn't discuss S-E-X at home. And I was too embarrassed to ask my older friends about making out with boys.

Public showers became easier, and I finally figured out both the dot next to my name in the gym class attendance book *and* the elastic belt. It was a handy gadget, actually, once one learned the tricky business of keeping pubic hair from getting caught in the buckle. Surprised looks appeared on many girls' faces when they sat down and the boys snickered. I mean, how could they know? They didn't have periods.

After asking about a flyer on the board in the locker room, I was handed a pamphlet about the Girl's Athletic Association (GAA). When someone gives me a pamphlet, it makes me think folks don't want to talk to me. I almost threw it back—until I saw the letter M in the school's colors. I read that you receive a letter after earning 1,000 points; and every 500 points thereafter was worth a bar. I had seen a few of those bars on school sweaters. It was a show of status and of accomplishment. That letter meant you were somebody and I wanted it. Badly.

Getting that letter became the most important goal I had ever set for myself. I signed up for everything I could: selling doughnuts at the games, handing out flyers at the door, joining the Booster Club. Everything. That following summer I was the pitcher on the girls' softball team. It felt great to belong to something and to be appreciated for a job well done. After years of being told that I couldn't do anything because I was a stupid girl, it amazed me I could do anything I set my mind on.

One afternoon, breathing hard, sweating, and feeling the aches and pains of running back and fourth on the court for an hour of basketball I felt a sudden euphoria. It was like my feet lifted off the floor as my body became lighter. I stopped, wondering if something was wrong with me. Within moments, the feeling dramatically eased off. From then on I pushed myself hard to obtain that "rush," but I never quite reached the level I had reached that first time. When I felt the rush, I pushed harder and longer. But it faded too fast. The few times I reached that "high" addicted me; when I practiced, it was more for the high than the game itself.

By the end of ninth grade I had 400 points toward my 1,000-point goal.

✻

Wax Myrtle—Discipline, instruction

I spent the summer before tenth grade riding around with noisy friends tooting car horns, shouting, hollering, and going to the drive-in to watch good-looking guys in their souped-up convertibles, guys who had their cigarette packs rolled up into the sleeves of their white T-shirts. It didn't matter that we were wallflowers; everyone still hooted and hollered. In tight skirts and oxfords a few of us walked to Cunningham's Drug Store for Lime Rickey's, swinging our behinds to a silent, sexy rhythm; but succeeding only in looking like moving distorted Popsicle sticks.

Throughout the year, new acquaintances came and went as my large dresser mirror became my altar, filled with pompoms, various club pens, pictures, and the school flag. Mr. Jones gave me the song, "Onward, Christian Soldiers" for my solo audition. By the end of the year, I had learned the left hand on the piano.

Being a physical late bloomer I didn't really enjoy making out with boys, but I did it anyway, lest I be accused of being "queer" or something. It grossed me out the first time one of them stuck his tongue into my mouth. He was so shocked when I roughly shoved him away; his tongue was still sticking out of his mouth. It was a lonely time for me. I would've liked the companionship of a young man, but there were too many who just wanted to "do it," and I didn't know what "doing it" meant.

I feigned interest in my little sisters and cooed over them whenever I took them to the kiddies' pool in the public park three blocks from our house. Trying to look provocative in Mom's one-piece, hand-me-down bathing suit, I lavishly smoothed on suntan lotion, though I stayed in the shade. I just wanted a little attention from the cute life guard. But all he wanted to do was hang around the older girls, wearing two-piece bathing suits.

My elderly friends had mostly died off by now and the boys of my tomboy days were in love or enraptured with someone else. One of the girls across the street was going steady with a boy who had joined the Air Force and they planned for a wedding after she graduated. Her older sister had gone…somewhere.

At home, there was the routine of not disturbing Dad when he came home from work. He ate his dinner alone at the kitchen table with his whiskey during weekdays. We walked on eggshells while he slept in on Sundays and drank whiskey and beer before noon on the weekends. The rest of us ate in the dining room. He ate steaks; we had vegetable soup with beef broth made from his steak bones. He had roasts; we had hash. The spaghetti Mom made in an aluminum five-gallon dishpan, breaking the noodles and letting them cook in the sauce, always tasted better the second day. Dad pretty much ruled over the television, as well. There was no one in the family to talk to or do things with. So I pretty much spent the summer before eleventh grade just wandering wherever my feet took me.

I had "Onward, Christian Soldiers" down pat, though I was still a little clumsy with the left hand, and I was singing well as an Alto, on my own. I would be ready by the end of the year for my tryout for First Choir. Within the first month of school, I met a new friend, Marie, who talked me into joining the Roller Skating Club. She hung out with two brothers. She dated the oldest, and I became friends with the youngest. Our favorite time was when the four of us went ice skating on the river.

I came to understand a little of what *family* was about when the mother of the two brothers joined us one evening by the river with a cooler full of hot dogs and cokes, plus chips and marshmallows. Having built a small bonfire next to the river, we huddled in each others arms while our meal cooked on a stick. My insides felt warm when I heard the fire crackling and smelled the wood smoke while watching a hotdog or marshmallow burning. Our noses ran in the cold crisp air and we would occasionally wipe them on our coat sleeves while waiting for a glimpse of a falling star in the dark sky. I was cold, numb, and not ice skating much, but what a delicious feeling I had down to my toes during those nights in the company of a family that never had a harsh word for each other and hugged easily. I was jealous of them, and at the same time, my heart was full for them.

My grades were slipping badly, so I knew I had to give up something. I couldn't give up secretarial homework. I couldn't play basketball for a living, and practice took up a lot of time, not to mention the actual games. I waited for as long as I could before telling my captain I would have to leave the team. It was the middle of the season and I figured Molly would be angry, but she told me she understood and would keep me on the team if I wanted to come back. That year, our team took first place in basketball and volleyball. Even though, I wasn't on the team the whole year, I still felt I had earned those medals and added them to my mirrored altar.

Mom styled my prom dress two different ways that year because I attended both proms, one as an usher at the Junior/Senior Prom. By then the boys had changed and looked different, not so dumb and were actually good-looking. Seeing my reflection in the mirror, wearing a dark pink, strapless chiffon, I realized I, too, had changed. I had hormones. And what was I supposed to do with this new physical feeling surging inside my body? I had no idea what it was and didn't know whom to ask.

I even shocked myself one afternoon when I deliberately dropped a book in front of Bill, the captain of our football team; I was dumbstruck and in love with him. He glanced at the book then at me and said. "Lady, you dropped your book," before stepping over it. Other students laughed while slapping Bill's back and ignoring me. Feeling foolish, I tucked the book into my arms while tucking my femininity into the far recesses of my soul.

They weren't wearing their robes, but the full complement of the First Choir was sitting in the tiered bleachers, waiting for me to start. The first of several soloists, I stood nervously at the grand piano. Mr. Jones sat off to one side of the choir. Taking a deep breath, I stepped around the bench, smoothed my skirt, and sat down, convinced I was going to forget every note I had spent three years memorizing.

When I glanced at Mr. Jones, he straightened his back, so I straightened mine. My voice came out small and barely audible; Mr. Jones shaped his mouth into an O, running his open hand up the front of his chest, so I sang louder. Then, imagining myself alone in the soundproof room, I played and sang the only song I knew how to play on the piano. The last note hadn't yet been hit when the choir stood up and applauded, signaling my acceptance into the First Choir. Even Mr. Jones stood applauding, smiling and nodding his approval. I floated home in elation that night, oblivious to everything around me. It didn't even matter there was no one to share it with.

I had babysat all that summer and saved what I could, looking forward to the choir's travels. I finally told Mom about the audition; she lightly responded that it was nice, but she would have to see about the traveling. Trepidation, mixed with anger, suspended my heartbeat at the mere thought of not being able to wear the burgundy robe I had worked so hard to earn. I thought up ways of sneaking out of the house. No one was going to stop me from wearing that robe...no one.

✻

On my first morning as a senior, I had just sat down in homeroom when I was given my class schedule. I froze, not believing my eyes. Time stood still as I reread it. In a heartbeat, I was truly convinced there was no God, no mercy of any kind in the world. In my junior year, with no prior knowledge of when it would be scheduled, I had signed up for my final secretarial classes, which would be held in the Vocational Education Building. In those last classes I would receive my on-the-job training in the workforce. To my horror, my secretarial training was scheduled from ten to noon; First Choir was ten to eleven. I hadn't moved in the fifteen minutes we had for homeroom and had not heard the bell. I continued to sit there, staring at the sheet of paper. Miss. Bell came over and asked if I was all right.

"No," I whispered in a constricted voice and rose to leave for my first class. But I didn't go to it.

I walked into the Music Room, and Mr. Jones was in his office. Spotting me standing next to the piano he walked out to greet me. He hesitated only a moment in his stride when he saw me with my eyes brimming with tears. I handed him my schedule. He read it then patted the seat next to him on the piano bench. He placed the schedule over the sheet music, and, in that moment, I knew. I remembered telling him about my secretarial classes; he knew this day would come.

Playing the piano, ever so softly, he said, "Lady, there comes a time in our lives when we are forced to make what we may think is a devastating, unfair choice."

"If you knew, why did you let me spend all that time on all those lessons?"

"Didn't you enjoy them? Didn't you learn more about music… about yourself?"

"Yes." My heart was breaking, and I felt a thin wall building itself around it at the same time. He knew what was going to happen. My mentor knew.

He continued in his soft, bass voice. "Music allows us to escape into a world apart from the one we are living in and softens the edges of a harsh reality. Sometimes it helps us to keep our sanity."

He was right. I remembered the mornings when I walked into the soundproof room angry and left twenty or thirty minutes later with a lighter heart.

"Did you have a harsh life? Is that why you teach music, to escape?" Tears flowed down my cheeks, and I let them dry on my hot cheeks. I listened to the music, my eyes glued to his hands moving on the keys, occasionally using his proffered handkerchief.

"I was blessed with wonderful parents. I teach music because I know what it can do, what I can do with it. I know how it can transform a dreary life. Once we learn the music within ourselves, nothing and no one can take that away from us."

"I wanted so much to wear the burgundy robe and travel." I sobbed.

"You can travel when you get out of school. As for the burgundy robe, didn't your peers stand up for you when you auditioned? How did that make you feel?"

"Proud. I could see myself in the robe, as one of them." I cried harder into the handkerchief. "I want it so badly."

"When your peers accepted you, you were given the burgundy robe, Lady. It's for you to wear around your heart when you feel the need to belong somewhere. The robe will always be there whenever you need it, and it can't be taken from you." He stopped playing and asked, "Please stand right there and sing for me."

And like a good little girl, I got off the bench and moved to the side of the opened grand and sang "Onward, Christian Soldiers." I understood what he had said. I always understood. But the wall was still around my heart. There was a moment of silence when I opened my mouth to ask for a note, but he raised his hand, signaling understanding. This time I followed him into his office where he reached for a pad on his desk and smiled.

While he was writing, I scanned the pictures behind his desk, and my eyes went to a picture of someone in a tuxedo facing a huge orchestra with upraised hands and holding a baton.

When he handed me the note, he saw where I was looking and said, "That was a long time ago," then glanced back to me before adding, "...and that was my choice. Lady, the soundproof room is yours whenever you need it. I know you will do well."

I shut his office door softly behind me just like I closed the door to my heart. I knew I would never step into to the Music Room again.

*

Vocational education was another world located just three blocks from the high school. And our high school vocational educational was a serious class. At graduation, we would receive a certificate booklet containing our picture, the courses we took and how many hours were in each course. This booklet would be signed by the head teacher, the principal, the superintendent of schools, and the state director of education. In fact, our class was one of the fifty high schools chosen nation-wide to test out the IBM electric typewriter before it went on the market. Through the job co-op, I worked at a Singer office typing address labels three hours a day in a small warehouse-type setting. After two weeks, I quit, wondering if secretarial work was what I really wanted.

GAA gave me my letter and I discovered I had missed a bar by only 100 points. On my letter were my class pin, Booster Club pin, library pin, roller skating pin, and the basketball and volleyball medals. Neither Mom nor I had any money for a blue sweater, so it remained on my mirror. I went to my proms wearing the same dress from the year before, but styled it differently.

Feeling more like a sister to all the boys coming to the house, I didn't think anything of Arnie coming around to show me how the seats in his VW reclined to a prone position. The following Friday, at the sock hop, I heard he told everyone he took me to the drive-in and we "did it." It was maddening. The boys smiled, the female jocks snickered and pointed and some of the prim-and-propers wouldn't talk to me. I left the dance and didn't go to another.

An Air Force recruiter came into our classroom about a month before graduation and spoke for nearly thirty minutes on the travel, education and experiences we would receive in the military. Not being able to afford college, I hadn't taken college prep courses in school, so the educational part hooked me. When I didn't pass the test, he suggested I try the Army, the branch of service that took those who couldn't do anything else or go anywhere else. When I said no thanks, he then referred me to the Navy. I passed that test and, at eighteen didn't need anyone's permission. Curiously, Mom was pleased at the educational aspect, also. Dad's comment was that he was in the Navy during World War II and got out as fast as he could. Nothing else was said. Graduating at 295 out of a class of 423 students, I readied myself for a new and exciting life.

✻

Anemone—Expectation

Listening to the clackity-clack of the train wheels on the tracks all night hypnotized me into numbness. The soft rocking motion of the sleeping compartment should have lulled me to sleep, but I was too nervous. Up before daylight, I looked out at the passing homes in large fields with their single lights on, perhaps in the kitchen. I imagined a woman cooking breakfast for her husband before sending him off to work.

Looking at those single lights in that vast darkness made me keenly aware of my loneliness and I began to doubt the wisdom of my joining the Navy. I had done impulsive things before, but not something that actually affected my life. Homesickness pervaded my heart as fear crept into my mind.

The train stopped at Bainbridge, MD, and the conductor stepped off, dropped my lone suitcase on the platform, then went over to the window and spoke to the man behind the bars. When he came back to me, he doffed his hat and said gently, "When you get on base, tell them you haven't eaten and they'll give you breakfast." Watching him walk away toward the train in his straight-back professional walk, I felt like my last friend had abandoned me. I picked up my bag, walked to the bench on the wooden platform, and sat down to wait. In the time it took to successfully chew off three finger nails, a dark blue car drove up. The driver got out and went to the window. When I was pointed out to him, he came over, picked up my suitcase, and flatly said, "Follow me."

Like a good girl, I followed him.

Passing the guardhouse as we drove onto the base, I was sure I was going to be locked up forever in a foreign land, and there was no one to help me escape. My heart raced. We passed several long barracks, reminding me of the government housing I lived in as a child. The buildings surrounded a huge blacktopped area the size of a football field, which I intuited it to be the center of the base. On this same field, I saw a couple of groups marching in formation. Everyone saluted each other and I couldn't tell the officers from the enlisted personnel.

Driving through a maze of streets, the driver finally stopped in front of one of the long barracks lining all of them. Opening my door, he took my suitcase and again flatly said, "Follow me."

I followed.

There was no getting acquainted with the Company Commander who, after greeting me, then told me to follow her as she walked up to the second floor. She walked into a cubicle containing two bunk beds along a wall with four lockers lined up across from them. Backing the lockers on the other side were four more lockers with the same bunk setup, only reversed. Outside walls had two very large windows, and inside walls, opened at the top, divided the cubicles from each other. Across the hallway were identical cubicles. After pointing out my locker and the bottom bunk to me, she silently led me to the mess hall.

Without introductions, we passed other girls sitting or waiting at long picnic-style tables in an enormous chow hall. I was instructed how to go through the chow line without making eye contact with the male personnel serving the food, yet make my choices known. The women at my table spoke very little during the twenty minutes allotted to eat our meal. We were then *marched* to another building and by ten a.m. were in the classroom where we would receive eight weeks of naval training. Having sped through the day, it was lights out after ten p.m. taps. I was so homesick in this alien world, I cried.

Our Company of twenty-five women was unique, ranging from barely five feet to six feet tall, every color and race imaginable, and from eighteen to thirty years of age. The open, room-size communal showers and heads (toilets) without doors provided a means for us to literally drop our inhibitions. In a very short time we shared advice, hair spray, family pictures, and clothing, everything intimate family members would share with one another. Three days after the initial start of boot camp, a notice on the bulletin board appeared regarding drill team tryouts the next day after evening mess. Applying, I passed.

The drill team taught me rhythm, teamwork, camaraderie, and the ability to focus every aspect of my body, and to do it in sync with my shoulders touching other team members. My face displayed my pride in the mirror every time I put the aglet on the shoulder of my uniform. I belonged to something that was shared with others of like mind as we marched in precision. Our feet stomping in loud unison, our singing, our in-sync movements gave me a sense of oneness with others I had never before experienced. I truly marveled at the oneness; breathed it, dreamed it, lived for it.

The drill team helped me through eight weeks of constant torture: the male personnel constantly stealing our underwear off the clothesline and teasing us with them; studying naval history, which I abhorred; and, as in high school, the younger females constantly huddling, giggling, and sharing gossip about everything and anyone.

The drill team, however, was the *only* unit good at marching in unison. After nearly three weeks of drilling as a Company, the Drill Instructor commanded us to left turn. Executing the turn we continued marching—right into the back wall. None of us thought to mark time (step in place), and we didn't have enough sense to just stop. Three columns marched into the wall, bunching, crunching, and giggling. And we nearly peed ourselves when the instructor blew her whistle to be heard.

Not only were we lectured by the Drill Instructor, who had suddenly transformed into one angry wet hen, clucking for over an hour, we also marked time the whole time she blew her damnable, shrilling whistle. Demerits, points assigned for every infraction of rules or regulations, were added to our files. Working off twenty-five demerits, I came to intimately know the electric buffer, using it three times on the drill hall floor the size of a city block, and cleaning the tiled floor of some of the heads with not a toothbrush, but a very,

very small brush. We lost our Company flag that day, representing our lowest dishonor. This also put us farther behind in obtaining the Achievement and/or Academic flags, with only five weeks of training left.

As a unit we were laughed at, not only by the male personnel in the mess hall, but by other recruit companies as well. We matured a little more as we took responsibility and worked at keeping the barracks clean between inspections. We practiced packing our duffle bags and their contents, folding everything into thirds and/or rolling it tight. We tested each other's bunks for tautness. We held study groups for our classes. We had a one-day liberty pass in the middle of boot training when we were taken by Navy bus to Lancaster, Pennsylvania. The rest of the time we spent marching, which I thoroughly enjoyed anyway, and working or studying.

⁎

Parsley— Useful knowledge

We also had a few reservists doing their annual two-week training. On my first mid-watch, I had a thirty-five-year old reservist veteran with me as the Senior Watch. With a flashlight in each hand (fear of the dark), I was walking down the gangway (hallway) when I heard noises toward the end the barracks on the second deck (floor). Slowly approaching the noise, I shined the flashlights on two girls. The one on the bottom bunk, on her stomach, was massaging the front of my roommate, who was on the floor. They gruffly whispered for me to turn off the flashlights. Not giving it another thought, I turned away and continued the rest of my round. When I got down to the quarterdeck, the reservist asked if everything was clear. I responded, "Yes, but you know…" and related what I had seen.

The reservist immediately got up from her chair and went up to the second deck, coming back ten minutes later. She went to a phone in the other office where I heard her calling our Company

Commander before she closed the door. When she came out a few minutes later, she looked at me as though she didn't quite know what to say before asking gently, "Do you know what a lesbian is?"

"No," I replied, and got no farther because the Commander rushed onto the quarterdeck (the first room entered when walking into a military building) looking as though she hadn't gone to bed and like she was very upset. I barely had time to salute before she curtly told me to stay on duty. She and the Senior Watch disappeared into the other office.

The door closed, I had no idea what was going on, but like a good girl full of all kinds of questions about lesbians, I stayed on duty. When they came out minutes later, the Commander left with a curt nod in response to my salute. The reservist turned to me and motioned for me to sit. When she got through explaining to me facts of life I was sure even my mother didn't know, I was dumbfounded. I don't know at what point my mouth had dropped open.

"What else don't you know?" she asked in a sisterly voice.

Aghast, I asked, "There's more?"

She then explained to me where babies came from, how they got there, and how they got out. In my head popped the image of the book about women and babies that Mom kept hiding from me when I was about ten. Gym class in high school hadn't shown this kind of film. Sitting and talking with the reservist was a stark reminder that I did not have an older sister, and it deepened my loneliness. I also knew she had saved me a great deal of grief by explaining the birds and the bees to me. If anyone else in my Company had learned of my ignorance, I would have been teased unmercifully.

When I got to my cubicle, my roommate wasn't there. Thinking of her conjured up the image of the other girl massaging her, except I now knew she hadn't been massaging her. The next morning at reveille, I was the first one to hit the deck. No one had to shake me awake as they had in the past. The thought of that other girl in my bunk… By morning chow, the rumor had spread about the two girls—not by me. After evening chow, our Company Commander mustered us in our barracks and informed us that the two girls had been discharged, and then she lectured us about what was and was not tolerated.

Part of our training was circling around an Olympic-size pool using the inflated legs of our wet dungarees as a flotation device. I had to do it three times because my dungarees deflated twice before I reached my starting point. We also had to jump off the Pink Elephant, a twenty-foot pink diving tower, and rise to the surface in a certain amount of time. A recruit did not get out of Navy boot camp without passing the water tests. Her first failure would set her back two weeks and put her into another Company; a second failure would mean discharge. Fear of water proved a bit tricky for me to pass. Also, an extreme and aggressive exercise routine was required for graduation. Enjoying the exercises, my body firmed up fast.

The weeks sped by as we polished mirrors into the tops of our Mickey Mouse shoes, learned to press our dark wool suits twice a week—never mind the over-90 degree temperatures—and tried our best to hold on to our light blue uniforms. They managed to disappear, and not always by the hands of the male animals across the compound. The women argued then made up and shared things again. The closer graduation day came, the more anxious we became because we hadn't yet received our Company flag back.

The day before graduation, we had our sea bag inspection. Not even size 32A and 36C bras neatly folded in the same sea bag got pass the inspectors. Only three Outstandings were given, and I was one of them. We received Outstanding for our white-gloved inspection of the barracks, done while we were in class. We also had our uniform inspection. Only two were awarded Outstanding WAVES—I had a dent in my tie. This enraged me because we were inspected by a woman who looked as though she had slept in her uniform and combed her hair with an egg beater. When I tried to protest, my Company Commander coughed. In my peripheral vision I caught her shaking her head. That night we were given our Company flag, along with the Achievement and Academic flags.

With the graduation ceremony in the afternoon, the morning quickly took on the atmosphere of a wedding day. Expectations of the day created chaos rather than order. Pantyhose somehow got switched. Makeup smeared. Everyone cussed out someone else. Above the din we all heard a different whistle blown and someone shouted, "Man aboard." Women scattered behind their locker doors faster than the drop of an eyelash. We heard our Company Commander laugh before she called out loudly, "Ten hut."

She marched down the gangway between two rows of 54 half-dressed women in various stages of disarray, from smeared lipstick, to pantyhose half on, hair in curlers, one shoe on and one shoe off standing at attention; well, as much at attention as they could achieve. One recruit caught sight of the recruit across from her and giggled.

By the time the Commander ended her slow walk to the end of the line, we were all relaxed, laughing, and pointing at each other. Her good deed accomplished, our Commander came to the center and showed us her new whistle. She then told us to take a deep breath and finish dressing. The recruits spent the rest of the morning greeting and visiting with their families. I enjoyed watching the visitors gleam with pride as they looked upon their daughters and asked them to parade in their uniforms. Those of us with no visitors went back to our bunks and silently finished packing our duffle bags. Sometimes, there are no words when the heart hurts.

It was the proudest moment of my life when our drill team marched our routine in front of the brass. When our Company stomped our feet that very first time to signal our turn to pass in revue, a curious silence fell over the field. Normally our Base Commander, commissioned Captain during the ceremony, stood at attention when the units of recruits passed. You could hear soft gasps when our peripheral vision caught her saluting *us* as we passed in front of her. Right next to her stood the saluting Secretary of Defense, our guest speaker, and next to him our Company Commander, also saluting. People were honoring me as a part of a unit. I belonged. I was somebody.

Snapdragon—Deception

Mom insisted I wear my uniform to show me off to everyone. My brothers and sisters oohed and aahed, Dad said I looked nice, and my aunts fussed over me. Yes, it was a very good feeling, but I wanted to get back to base. I knew once the novelty wore off, everything would go back to normal. Having been assigned to six months of IBM school on the same base but at a different location, I looked forward to learning a vocation at which I could make a good living in civilian life and secure my future.

I arrived back on base with more luggage than the first time; bringing back with me what most represented my life. I had left behind the things around my mirror. Feeling years beyond them, I had tucked them into the dresser drawers.

My new barracks had the same-size cubicles but they actually had doors and two women shared a room, not eight. The single cots were separated bunk beds. We each had a dresser, a locker, and a lot more room, with each room taking on the personalities of the residents. Walking into mine for the first time, I nearly knocked down my new roommate, Jonnie. Jonnie was the exact opposite of me. With pretty black hair, she was bold, animated, and very outgoing. Laughing at the near mishap, we partnered in a very short time. She reminded me of Jennie, but without the boobs. Jonnie didn't put on airs to get noticed because she just didn't care. She did what she could get away with because she thought it fun to find out if she could. Sometimes her audacity frightened me and at the same time excited me.

Since we were in the same IBM class, we were together day and night. She knew how to attract boys, except some of them were men—over 21. We went to the Enlisted Men's Club and, when invited, to the NCO Club. Often we would sit in the bar with a ten-cent glass of beer, making it last for nearly two hours, and waiting for a sailor to pay. Jonnie smoked, so I learned to smoke. Bad habits were easily learned and readily enjoyed. And then there was that other thing—doing *it*.

One night a very young NCO took me off base. We were making out in the front seat when he went down on his knees and started to unbutton his pants.

"What are you doing?" I asked, truly puzzled.

First staring at me, then out the window, he finally asked in a voice that reflected a different puzzlement, "What do mean? Don't you wanna do it?"

"Do what?" came out of my mouth before I realized what he

had said. Then I remembered from high school some of the other kids "doing it," and the reservist's pep talk about the facts of life.

Getting up while buttoning his pants, he said over and over, "I have a virgin. I don't believe I have a virgin." Driving back to base, he occasionally glanced in my direction, shook his head and repeated, "A virgin."

I got out of the car in front of the barracks and never saw him again.

About two weeks later, Edouard, attending Officer's Training School, approached me for a weekend date in New York City. Now, I had never been to New York before and told him yes. Thinking he was driving us, I was really surprised when we took the base bus to the Greyhound station. Edouard explained, "When I get through with OTS, I'm going to Annapolis. I can't see having a car until there's truly a need for one." It made sense to me.

Conversation was sketchy. He asked questions about me and I answered them. I had never been alone with a man for that long by myself. And he *was* a man because he told me he was nearly twenty-five and of French heritage to boot. When the bus stopped in New York City, he took my suitcase and hailed a taxi to take us to the Manhattan Hotel. It never occurred to me to wonder about the sleeping arrangements. In my mind, we were going sightseeing, and hadn't thought any farther. In the room, I put on the white dress I wore at my high school graduation, but somehow the dress didn't feel the same. Scrutinizing myself in the mirror, it fit tighter in my chest and in my hips, and I wondered where the Popsicle-stick body had gone. My waist had slimmed down as well, I noticed.

When we got to the street, I was glad we were walking because I wanted to look into the store windows. We held hands as we walked to the Ripley's Believe It or Not! Museum, then on to the famous Peppermint Lounge for a drink. I couldn't understand why it was so famous since it was so small. In fact, we had passed it twice because the entrance door so obscure. I was puzzled when a man crossed the street, touched his hat brim, and nodded to Edouard, while smiling. When I asked why he had done that, Edouard responded, "It was his way of saying I'm with a very pretty woman."

Me! A woman! And pretty! I grinned so broadly for so long that my face hurt. Several hours later, in the hotel room, he ordered dinner and a bottle of champagne. I sat on the bed feeling pretty and pretended I was married to a wealthy man. While we talked in soft tones, someone knocked on the door and a voice said, "Room Service."

"Room service?" I asked, wondering when he had made the arrangements.

Edouard smiled and opened the door. It was just as I had seen in the movies. I couldn't believe my eyes. A man in black plants, vest, white shirt and a black bowtie wheeled in dinner on a table with a rose on the white tablecloth, silver covers, cloth napkins, and the champagne in a bucket of ice. He even had a towel over his arm. Edouard signed a piece of paper, then turned and smiled at me when the man in the penguin suit left. Still in the wonder of the moment, I lifted the silver lids and admired over the rose. And, so help me, I giggled like a silly school girl when the cork flew across the room and the champagne spewed out, just like in the movies.

Dinner was delicious, and the champagne bubbles enthralled me when they tickled my nose. Edouard, sitting next to me, kissed me. And this was different. He kissed me a long time, and I felt a warmth rise up through my body. He took my glass and placed it on the cart. My groin muscles ached and I was damp between my legs, but I wasn't scared. Never before had I been held the way Edouard held me, speaking softly as he ever so gently and slowly removed my dress.

Experiencing for the first time this flood of mixed emotions and the physical feelings in my body, I surprised myself when a moan escaped my throat. I surrendered myself to this exquisite world of soft embraces in the arms of a man who wasn't hurting me and appeared to genuinely care. Edouard took his time undressing me. I quickly discovered that this rapid breathing was very different from the rapid breathing of playing basketball. Awed by his gentle touches and caresses, I couldn't get enough of them.

He penetrated me while I was still laying flat on the bed. In a deep, breathless voice, he said "Lady, lift your knees up and bend them." I did and oh, my, my, my. Everything after that was intuitive.

The next morning I was sore and a little embarrassed when Edouard kissed me lightly. It was then I saw blood on the sheet and became concerned. He quickly pulled the top sheet over it and told me, "Women do that sometimes when they make love," and lightly kissed me again.

So this is what "doing it" is all about. And it's called lovemaking. Nice! Really nice! I was hooked and wanted more. Smiling, Edouard said we had to catch the bus, and we hadn't eaten breakfast yet. He checked the mirror to make sure everything on his uniform was straight and taut and his few ribbons were in place. When he put on his hat, I thought him a handsome man. He then opened the door, grabbed our small suitcases, and crooked his right arm for me. Looking back at the rumpled bed and the remnants on the food cart, I sighed. For one night I had been loved for me, and if lovemaking was what it took for a man to hold me like that and to appreciate me…

The bus ride back to the base was quiet, but I couldn't keep my hands off of Edouard's arm. I thought that touching him would bring back the same exquisite emotions I had felt the night before. I discovered I'd need a lot more than just touching him. When I asked if we could go back to New York the following weekend, he told me he had spent his whole month's paycheck. Aghast, I felt my face redden at my ignorance, and I apologized for my boldness. He gently patted my hand and smiled, making me feel like a silly child.

When we got back to the base, he put my luggage on the quarterdeck, kissed my cheek and told me I was beautiful and walked away. When I entered our room, Jonnie looked at me, clapped her hands, laughed, and squealed, "You lost your cherry! Marvelous."

Looking into the mirror, I saw my face glowing, but was curious at the slight depression I felt. Knowing now what men wanted, and how to use my assets, I had a new sense of power. I decided to use it, often.

✻

IBM school was enjoyable. Wiring the accounting boards was engrossing and challenging and I rarely made mistakes. However, I couldn't pass the tests. The Chief of our department didn't help my frustration any by inviting me to clean his house on the weekends. I had heard that some of the other girls who were invited to "clean his house" did so in a French maid's uniform. That didn't make sense to me. Why dress up in a short, fancy dress to clean?

I became serious with John, an NCO, and dated him for several weeks. We even spoke of getting married. I got drunk in a club one night and met John's best friend, Frank. That night was the first time I blacked out while on my feet. Two hours later, Frank handed me my underwear. At first I refused, until I realized I wasn't wearing any. I was angry with Frank on the way back to the base, and he begged me not to tell John about our date. Date, indeed.

Six weeks had passed and I discovered I had missed my period. I told no one but John that I thought I might be pregnant. He flatly declared it wasn't his.

"What do you mean it's not yours? You're the only one I've have been with."

"No, I'm not. Frank told me you two were together. Besides, there are two things you should know," he continued. "One, I'm married and have been for nearly three years, and two, I'm not able to have children. I'm sterile."

I couldn't move, even when he walked away I still stood there until Jonnie came up. "My God, Lady. What did he say to you?"

I didn't have to answer. Tugging my arm, she turned me around and walked me back to the barracks. I couldn't cry. I sat on my bed while Jonnie chattered on and on about how we were going to start over at new bases.

The Chief asked me one more time before the final exam to clean his apartment, and one more time I refused. I didn't pass my finals and, therefore, didn't pass the school. Given the choice of two bases, I chose to transfer to Charleston, SC. Jonnie had received her orders for the same base, but my orders had come in the morning mail, and I knew I would leave before her.

The Chief called me into his office shortly after and informed me that nothing got through his office without his approval, and Jonnie and I weren't going to transfer together. We were trouble together.

I waved my orders in front of him and said triumphantly, "Well, Chief, it doesn't look like the brass think you're so hot and there's nothing you can do about it." I stomped out of his office, slamming the door.

It struck me then why I hadn't passed, but I couldn't prove it. Something hot ignited in the pit of my stomach and internal flames rose within me. I realized I had been angry for a long time.

✻

With two days to go, I packed my trunk just for something to do, anything to relieve the numbness in my heart. For the rest of those two days, I wondered what there was about me that made men so sure they could use me then discard me. I even asked Jonnie. She stared at me and said nothing, but I could tell she was worried.

Two days, one trunk, and three suitcases later, sitting in the train station, I thought of the nice train conductor the first morning I arrived on base nine months ago. A humorless chuckle escaped me when memories of my naiveté rushed in. It felt like a lifetime ago. Hurting deeper than I had ever imagined, I wanted out of the Navy. It, too, had lied to me with promises of an education I couldn't actually use. The uniform represented a sham. Sick at heart, depressed and not really caring about anything, I wearily rose from my chair when I heard my train announced.

*

Monkshood—Danger is near

"You can go see the doctor this afternoon and use the rest of the day to settle in. We can talk more tomorrow when you come on duty," my new barracks officer replied to my question.

The women's barracks resembled a small resort, with wings on either side of the very large quarterdeck. My second-floor room shared a bathroom with the adjoining room. I hesitated to put my luggage next to the empty bed. Everything was immaculate and neat.

I don't know who I expected for a roommate, but it wasn't the woman who walked into the room. She was blonde, my height, and First Class. She shook my hand, and introduced herself as Sharon. She reminded me of the types that eats apples daily; reads a book a week; wears a sweater when it's cool; and sports dark-framed eyeglasses—which she actually did wear. I scarcely gave her another thought.

Assigned to the barracks as Senior Watch, I cleaned the barracks for weekly inspection, manned the quarterdeck during the day, and took turns with five other women for four-hour watches beyond the day job. My period came a week after my transfer, and I had to stay in bed during the first three days because it hurt so badly. I became concerned when I bled for a whole week, but blew it off to the stress of transferring.

Jonnie came two weeks later and was assigned a room right below me. We were close friends for about two weeks. She had changed in the short time before she had transferred to the new base. She became quiet and a little too staid for me. I continued to go to the hot spots and party all night long, dating anyone who would go out with me. New cocktail dresses were costly, so I bought a sewing machine and made my own. I bought satin dress shoes and dyed them to match the dresses.

One morning I came into my room still dressed in evening clothes. My roommate, whom I rarely saw, asked if we could talk. "Sure," I answered and plopped down on my bunk.

"Lady, something's happened to you. You seem to be on a suicide mission—"

"My life is none of your damn business, so just leave me the hell alone," And I went into the bathroom and vomited.

I rinsed my face, towel drying it. The mirror reflected a haggard old, yet young, woman. I noticed lines around my eyes that hadn't been there a few weeks ago. I was angry all the time and didn't know why. What I did recognize, again, was my great need to keep moving, to stay in front of *it* before *it* caught up to me. I didn't know what it was, just that it terrified me.

There was a very large round table in the Enlisted Men's Club that seated twelve people. At six in the evening, it was my habit to sit at the table with eight men and leave three chairs vacant. By six-thirty those three chairs would be filled by naval or marine personnel. We discussed everything from politics to economics to philosophy. Then, as always, we discussed men, women, and sex. There was one particular Chief who adopted me as one would adopt a stray puppy. He made sure I was kept safe from those around the table, including keeping the foul language to a minimum.

Over several weeks, he taught me lessons about another set of rules regarding men and women. I learned how to use my "feminine wiles" to make a man feel good, and I used these lessons, often, after much testing. The Chief never knew I also learned the power of manipulating others by using their weaknesses. Jewelry and gifts from homesick men were nothing to me. I became their mother, sister, friend, or lover. I was anyone they wanted me to be as long as it got me off the base and into the parties. But I was never happy at the loud, raucous functions that usually ended just before dawn.

A problem arose that totally perplexed everyone, especially me. Walking into town one day, feeling truly depressed, I crossed the street, stepped onto the sidewalk, then…nothing. I woke up in the emergency room looking up into the eyes of a good-looking, young doctor.

"Am I all right?" I asked, afraid to move for fear I had broken something. Noting that nothing hurt, I tried to sit up.

"Don't do that yet. We want to get some information"

I couldn't answer their questions because I didn't know what had happened; I was walking, then I was in the hospital. A few hours later, tired and very confused, not to mention scared for fear something was really wrong with me, I was escorted to the psychiatric ward of the hospital without any explanations. During the next week, doctors and staff took x-rays, did physical exams, and drew blood and fluid samples, including a spinal tap. I found out later they even gave me IQ tests. All the while, they asked me a million questions regarding my health, mind, and background, over and over again.

I barely remember my time in the Psychiatric Ward, but I do remember a weird incident. My psychiatrist came into my room one afternoon then discovered he didn't have the key to unlock the door to get out. Within minutes he had climbed the door, which had no doorknob, by using his fingers in the crevices between the door and the jam. Moments later, a nurse and two male nurses had him in his straight jacket and hauled him off. I don't know when I started laughing.

A younger, good-looking psychiatrist came in the next day and told me all the tests had come back negative, and all x-rays were normal. What surprised me were the three IQ tests. I hadn't known what they were or why there were three. I just took them—one being all essay. All three scores came back higher than I could have ever imagined. So high, in fact, that I mistrusted them.

One thing I painfully noted while in the hospital was the lack of visitors. No one came except Jonnie, who came once. It was very evident to me after I was released that something wasn't normal with me and I didn't know what it was, or what to do about it. And for the life of me I didn't know when things had changed. As one day melded into another, my depression worsened as did my deep anger. I didn't care whom I dated and many nights I drank myself sober from six in the evening until four a.m. breakfast. I slept little, and when I did, it was not a restful sleep because nightmares woke me. My work performance got worse because I couldn't concentrate and overnight, I grew to hate my job.

A few weeks later I was crying in the bathroom, holding a razor blade in my right hand. I had already cut two gashes in my left wrist and was cutting the third when Jonnie walked in, took one look, and ran out screaming. I ran out in the hallway, laughing and showing my wrist to everyone. I stopped when I felt an odd weakness in my legs. Things went black before I dropped like a sack of flour. When I came to I was back in the psychiatric ward of the hospital again—in the same room.

On cue, a good-looking doctor walked in and sat on the edge of the bed. "You've been here before," he stated congenially in his best bedside manner.

Raising my left hand and putting it under my head, I looked at him and smirked, "Well, give you a star. Did you make that up or did you read it somewhere?" I got out of bed; not caring that my hospital gown exposed my bare ass.

At times, I mulled over what was wrong with me and why I had turned into a depressed, morose, female who wanted to kill herself. Where had I turned on life's path, and just what kind of path was

I on? What had caused me to turn? Angry, tired, I felt like worn-out shoe leather on the bottom of a shoe. The interview went as I expected, and the doctor left disappointed. The questions had been different this time. I was put on Librium and discharged from the hospital a few days later.

*

Orange Lily—Hatred, dislike

My dark thoughts didn't get any better. I smiled a lot and spoke less and less. Jonnie and I rarely talked, and my roommate left the room if I was there for any length of time. I stopped worrying why people treated me differently. It was their problem, not mine.

A few days later, Jonnie and I decided to go AWOL. While packing my suitcases, my roommate asked if I was transferring. Never having claimed to be intelligent, I responded, "Nope, going AWOL." Picking up my two suitcases, I went to the quarterdeck and waited for my ride. Jonnie went out the back. Like I said, I wasn't very smart. As I got into the car, the Senior Watch yelled out to me that she had called the MPs; my roommate stood beside her. I shouted an expletive and waved, feeling a sense of freedom in fleeing from the hell of my life.

Two days on the road, and we were in a vehicle driven by a short man with another one in the back in a hip cast. Not getting any brighter, I mentioned to the man with the cast that we were AWOL. We went to their apartment thinking we were safe and were offered their L-shaped sofa for a rest before dinner. We accepted gratefully.

Coming up out of a dead sleep, my eyes flew open. Staring at the ceiling, I didn't hear anything, but I sensed something was very wrong. Five men lolled around the room, either leaning or sitting. I looked to the short man, the owner of the apartment, with a question on my face.

"We want a sex party," he said, smirking.

I said, "Come on, Jonnie. We're out of here," and I got dressed. Being the smarter one, Jonnie had kept her street clothes on.

Our suitcases hastily packed, we were walking toward the front door when the short man opened up the patio door and casually said, "You can leave this way."

We slid our suitcases behind us as we cautiously crept down the long, steep lawn to a four-lane highway. It was our third night without sleep; I felt punch-drunk sitting on my suitcase on the center line of the highway.

With a cigarette lighter in my hand, I was trying to read a road map when two bright headlights, straddling the double yellow line, moved up behind me. Turning to look, I was blinded and hollered, "Hey, asshole, turn off the damn lights." I heard a car door open then a man's footsteps walking toward me. Silhouetted against one of the headlights was a cop in uniform—with a billy club.

No questions, no hello. The silhouette just said, "Where's your girlfriend?"

It was a curious question for my sleep-deprived brain. I hadn't thought about Jonnie until then, and I just couldn't fathom where she could have gone until I saw a road to the right of where I was sitting.

"How about up there?" I pointed, and went back to my map.

By this time a second set of footsteps had walked over to where I sat, except the uniform on this one wasn't dark. It was a pretty Air Force blue. My gaze slowly scanned the figure from the mirrored-top shoes, past the two stars on the collar, to the general's face. His look ordered me to not say a word, but it didn't stop me from snickering. God, I was tired and getting number and dumber by the minute. The general muttered something before looking up. Both of us watched the police officer approach us, holding Jonnie by the arm. Neither of them offered to carry our suitcases as they escorted us into the back of the police car.

Jonnie sat quietly as I snickered and snorted, past caring and not able to control myself. The cop said nothing, but the general…he kept punching his left palm with his right fist. I got the distinct impression he wanted very badly for my face to be in his left palm and the thought made me laugh louder. Bordering on hysterics by that time, I still allowed my dull brain to register that I was on the verge of walking over a very dangerous threshold, and so I tried to sober up. The general slapped his right fist into his left palm harder. I turned my head and stifled my laughter in the upholstery of the squad car. Jonnie said nothing. She just kept looking at me like I was a stranger.

Arriving at the base, my dragging feet stumbled across the quarterdeck. Glancing around the room, I noticed the two gorilla-sized MPs at parade rest, looking straight ahead, on either side of the door. I had never seen anything like that before. I heard shouting when another MP, the one I assumed was in charge, came out of the back room with the general following him.

"What are you going to do with these two bitches?" the general shouted.

The MP, his short height barely meeting the minimum requirement, said in a soft tone, "The matter will be attended to, sir. Their base has been notified and we are waiting for their escorts."

My foggy brain registered what he said and I was about to ask how he knew who we were when the general, near my ear, broke through my thoughts with, "They should be taken out and shot. Women aren't worthy enough to suck the maggots out of a dead nigger's ass—"

Everything went black.

When the darkness faded, my vision expanded, and the room came into view, I saw the general on the floor behind the short MP, wiping blood from his nose and mouth. What struck me as odd was that I was looking down on them. My body was numb, but my brain of mush somehow registered that the two gorillas at the door had me pinned up between them and raised me about two feet off the floor. I blinked my eyes at the MP, totally confused about what had just happened to the lights, who had hit the general, and why I was trussed up between the two MP's.

I began to think I had entered a *Twilight Zone* episode when the short MP walked over to me, looked up, and asked, "Are you all right?"

"I think so," was all I could manage and I wasn't even sure about that.

He nodded to the two gorillas, and they dropped me. I was beyond pain, and more fatigued than I had ever been in my life. Not having the energy to move, I just stayed on the floor. He brought over a chair for me and quietly said, "Your friend is in the holding room sleeping on a cot. A plane is coming to take you back to your base."

I sat silently staring at the floor, remembering the Hispanic girl. I used to visit one of the submarines during the weekend. The men were like my brothers to me when they showed me around the sub. I had always felt safe with them, as safe as I felt with my family. While I had been on weekend watch, the Captain of the Watch on board ship found this young, Hispanic woman willingly being gang-banged in the galley (kitchen). When the admiral caught wind of it, all women were banned from all the ships and u-boats. I had gone down to the sub the following weekend and was told why I could no longer go aboard. I confronted her about the incident, and she laughed and spat in my face because she had heard I was an Indian.

I blacked out.

The next thing I knew she was sliding down the Coke machine, blood trailing from the back of her head where she had hit it on the bottle opener. An ambulance took her for an overnight stay at the hospital; she suffered a mild concussion.

Sitting on the floor, I wondered if the same thing was going on here.

"I've never seen a black button on a woman before." The short MP's comment brought me out of my stupor.

"What's a black button," I asked in a voice I could barely push out of my throat.

"A black button is when the soul momentarily leaves the body and the eyes turn black." He got up from his chair to get some coffee. "How long have you been abused?" he asked, handing me a mug.

Dropping my gaze to my cup, I replied, "I don't know what you're talking about." My defensive tone sounded weak, even to me. I truly didn't know what he was talking about, though a tiny bit of recognition clicked within me. But I couldn't think straight and my soul ached.

"The men you were with tonight are MP's," he said quietly.

"They wanted a sex party and we didn't," I whispered hoarsely.

"It wouldn't have mattered. If you'd had the sex party, they would have turned you in anyway. One of them is very gung-ho."

I assumed he meant the one who owned the apartment. The MP's tone was soft and gentle and, for the first time in what seemed like eons, I wanted to cry. I was barely able to sit up by then, so he gently took my hand, then my arm and walked with me into an empty holding room. Taking my cup, he helped me onto the cot, and I don't remember my head hitting the pillow. I dreamed a dead man's dream.

⁂

Cyclamen—Resignation & goodbye

Back at our home base, we were placed on restriction until our hearings. Two weeks later, Jonnie received a hand slap out of her disciplinary hearing for her first offense. Two weeks after her hearing, I was given a Captain's Mast (a full hearing by a judge with a WAVES representative) because of my previous disciplinary hearing two months earlier. I had gone on leave and came back AWOL because of food poisoning. The Captain's Mast was also for going off base during the month's restriction after I came back from being AWOL. I had actually called in and mustered myself instead of the watch doing it, but I was the only one who thought it funny.

I was given another thirty days' restriction, but this time with an escort every time I left the barracks, and with a chit signed by each person in the office I visited, coming and going. I no longer had to report to my duty station because the discharge my psychiatrist had submitted on my behalf would be ready at the end of the thirty days. I lost my Seaman's stripe and was fined.

Just when I thought I was going to get a month's vacation, I was told I had to be up at reveille, in bed by taps, and muster every hour on the hour, in uniform. I was also told that another infraction of any rule or regulation of my restriction would land me in Parris Island, a military prison. I wondered why the Air Force general was never mentioned and assumed it had something to do with the short MP. There was something in his nature, an element of good.

When I had been on restriction for a few days the Captain of the barracks rose from her chair as I was passing through the quarterdeck. With a rancor in her voice, she said, "I'm going to have to take your uniform and insignia."

Surprised, I stopped and stared at her. "By whose authority?"

"I want your uniform. You're not fit to wear it." She threw the words at me like she wanted them to be knives.

That made me mad. Nothing had been said at my hearing about a dishonorable discharge where they stripped your uniform. Deliberately and slowly I paced each step toward her until I came within a few inches of her face. In a voice saturated with hatred, I said, "Take it off me, bitch." She didn't respond and simply sat down. But from that time on she was there for every hour I had to muster. She badly wanted me out of there, preferably in Parris Island.

During my first two weeks with Sharon, I discovered my roommate was a nice person, almost too nice for my comfort. I thought her above me in all respects and that she was everything I wished to be. She was smart, pretty, able to converse with anyone, never angry, didn't cut anyone down—everyone liked her. She came back from the doctor one day, and I asked if she was ill. She responded that she was getting married soon and had the doctor cut her hymen.

"Your what?" I asked, not having a clue what she was talking about. When she explained what a hymen was, I thought of Edouard.

Sharon also, one day, brought out a tampon. When I asked what it was, she explained where and how it was inserted and why. I then asked her how she peed after plugging herself up with a tampon. Her mouth dropped open, and, we were suddenly enveloped in a balloon of silence. For just a hairsbreadth moment, we were in a small ball that seemed to float barely above the floor. In the next moment we were back on the floor and the noise from the hallway invaded our room again.

She asked in an astonished voice, "Are you serious?" Then looked at me as though she suddenly understood how the world turned on its axis.

I asked Sharon where she had learned about tampons. "In the grocery store," she responded before quietly ducking into the bathroom.

It had never occurred to me to look for anything other than the pads. I spent the next two weeks learning other things left out of my gender education, like douching and checking my breasts for lumps, and much more.

With nothing to do during the day except get dressed in my uniform, which I hated beyond reasoning, my mind wandered over the past fifteen months of my life. Time and time again I tried to understand where my anger had come from, whom or what caused it, and especially why I was aging so fast. There was something elusive always floating among my thoughts, but for the life of me, I couldn't grab hold of it. I was frustrated enough to throw things. I asked Jonnie to get some beer and sneak it up to me.

With my two beers in hand, I went into my closet and guzzled them. In a few minutes I felt better but lightheaded. I wasn't an alcoholic, and I wasn't sure if I wanted to be numb or if I wanted to feel. What I did know was that something had gone wrong since I transferred to this base, and I didn't know what it was, or even if it was more than one thing gone awry. I wrote home less and less. I had to chuckle when I remembered a letter Mom had sent me the first time the hospital staff notified her. She had written, "I know you can handle it." What a joke. Some days I was scared because I didn't know what *it* was. Again, the *it*, but a different *it* this time.

Most of the time, I just plain didn't care. More and more, my thoughts leaned toward suicide as the easiest way out. I didn't want to die, but there seemed to be no other solution. I tried talking to people, but was either laughed at, ignored, or medicated. Some just turned around and went back the way they had come.

When it came time for me to leave the base, the Captain was waiting on the quarterdeck. She had taken the liberty of calling a cab. In the doorway as I was going out, she stuck out her hand and for a moment I thought she wanted to make amends. "Your ID card," she said.

Looking up at her, I saw she was smiling. I calmly put my suitcases down, reached into my purse, and took out my ID card. There was no blackout as I grabbed her blouse, ripping off a button, and shoved my ID card down her bra. Pushing her against the doorjamb, I hissed, "I'd have shoved it up your ass, but it's too damned tight."

Riding the cab past the guardhouse for the last time, I thought of the first time I had passed a guardhouse when I was entering boot camp. It had been only sixteen months ago, but I felt I had traveled light years into a dark abyss, with nothing to show for my life's journey but an old face, a walled-up heart, a dead spirit, and a numbed body.

✳

Verbena—Pray for me

After paying the cab driver, I walked into my new apartment. I had been allowed a day's pass to find living quarters three days before my discharge. I slept the whole weekend and, on Sunday, having only a few bucks left, began to wonder what I was going to do for money. The kind woman up stairs must have had ESP because she came down with coffee, a roll, and a newspaper, and said to let her know if I needed anything else. She and her husband reminded me of the elderly neighbors of my childhood days.

My spirits picked up a little as I read through the want ads but were dashed after reading of only waitress jobs and secretarial positions. Mom was a waitress, so I didn't want to do that. And I, for sure, didn't want another typist job in a warehouse somewhere. My gaze landed on a short ad for a legal secretary, offering training for the right person. Getting dressed, I went up stairs and asked where I could catch a bus and which one would take me to town.

By the time I got home, I had two bags of groceries and a job. The next morning would be my first day as a legal secretary-in-training in a very small law office. For the first time since leaving home, I felt good about what I was doing. My high school training was going to pay off after all, and I didn't need the hellish Navy. Bus fare was a dime and cigarettes cost more in civilian stores, so I decided I'd walk the mile and a half to and from work. My money was low and I wouldn't be paid for another two weeks, but knew I could manage.

For two days of training, I typed legal documents, using words beyond my knowledge and vocabulary. My typing was rusty and got worse every time the secretary and the boss pointed out my mistakes. I was at my wits end by the time Friday came, my first day without the former secretary at my side. I could do nothing right and was really curious why I hadn't been fired. Then, when quitting time came, my boss asked if he could drive me home.

Red flags shot up. I hesitated only a moment before cooing, "Sure. It would be a nice relief from walking."

We stopped for a drink and small talk. By the time we had pulled up in front of my door, he had given me the old line about how his wife didn't understand him.

"Well, Mr. Woods, that's unfortunate because I do," I replied in a tired voice. "I don't think I'm going to work out as your secretary. You want more than I want to give." Feeling a hundred years old, I got out of his car and didn't look back. I didn't go to work on Monday, and I didn't go back for my paycheck, nor did he send it to me. By Monday afternoon I was working in a filthy diner for four dollars for an eight-hour day. By the end of the week I had cleaned the place, and more customers were coming in.

The owner, whom I had never met, had watched me all week and come Friday, introduced herself. She had round spots of bright rouge on her cheeks, deep red lipstick that came off on her teeth, and dark hair pulled back in a tight bun at the base of her head. Her beady eyes missed nothing. I wasn't comfortable around her but it was okay—because she doubled my salary that day.

The customers came in and gawked, tried to pinch me or get friendly, and I wouldn't have any of it. After my third week, the owner took me to a booth in the back. In a syrupy voice she said I needed to get better acquainted with the customers. Any money they gave me was mine, after I gave her fifty percent. Now that was a first. I had never met a female pimp before. I laughed. I laughed out loud and she got mad.

"You're fired," she snarled through a twisted, lipstick-smeared mouth.

"Too late. I quit," I snapped and took off my apron.

While I was on my way to the door, one of the customers tried to pinch me, but I saw it coming. Before he could touch me, I smacked his hand so hard it hit the edge of the table. He cried out. I turned toward him, and, with my other hand, smacked his face as hard as I could. I was a strong-built woman. While I stood there, daring him to do more, he rubbed the back of his hand, his face turning a mottled red and his eyes brimming. The owner came over with two goons I'd never seen before.

"Forget it, bitch. I'm leaving this roach-invested dump." I narrowly missed another customer when I angrily shoved open the door.

The restaurant was several miles from my apartment, so I usually rode the bus. This time I walked, or rather I walked-ran, barely able to see for the tears running down my cheeks. That walk home was a blur.

When I got to my apartment, Jonnie was there with a male friend. Seeing my ugly mood, she excused herself and her friend, leaving her six-pack behind. The beer was gone in a short time and I felt better, still angry, but better. I noticed my Librium was nearly gone and went down to the corner store to call the base psychiatrist. He said he would be out the next week. I complained that there were only a couple days of pills left and was told I should have kept better track of them. Feeling like a berated child, I banged the receiver down. A tiny knot tightened in the pit of my stomach. No pills, no money, and the rent was due. Depression settled in and I slept the weekend away.

When the psychiatrist finally came, I had been three days without the pills and feeling miserable. He set them on the coffee table, and when I reached for them, he snatched them away. With deliberate emphasis he said, "Lady, you'll need to pay for these." Then he sat back on the couch, the pills in his hand and a tiny smile on his face.

Rage rose up from the core of my being, and I knew if it reached my brain, I couldn't control it. "Is that how you get your sex? Get women hooked then demand payment?"

They were stupid questions to which we both knew the answers, but I had to keep talking, had to keep moving, had to keep the rage down. I paced the floor, his smile was even broader. He had me, and he knew it. Or did he? Suddenly, I picked up the coffee table by the rim underneath and tossed it as hard as I could into his lap. His hand came up, but not in time. When the coffee table fell over onto the floor, bouncing till it righted itself on all four legs, the good doctor was holding a broken, bloody nose and one eye was already darkening.

Shoving the pills into his pocket, he growled "That's it, you fucking bitch. There will be no more." He made a movement, as though he was going to backhand me.

"Do it, you bastard," I growled and moved closer to him. "But you'd better make sure I don't get back up, you piece of slimy shit."

I glowered at him, daring him. I badly wanted him to hit me. I wanted a reason to beat him down, to stomp him into a pulp. Sixteen months of rage rose up like bitter gall in my throat. I wanted him dead.

He looked into my eyes and said nothing, but he backed away from me toward the door. Not taking his eyes off me, he reached behind, opened the door, and stepped out backwards. Then he all but ran to his car, still holding his nose.

The stilled silence drained me: I was spent. Suddenly, someone was pounding on my door and before I could reach it, I heard the landlord outside, demanding his rent money that was nearly a week late. My feet, as though bogged in a quagmire, dragged my body into the bedroom. There was nothing left of me but a shell.

I slept until about eleven that night. With nothing in the

refrigerator to eat, I got dressed and went out for a walk. I used to enjoy the night air, the coolness washing over the earth, moving warm fragrances around while I tried to discern the scents. Tonight, the night air suffocated me. There was nothing, no senses or feelings, no joy, nothing but an empty shell.

I noticed something black in the distance and walked toward it. A river with man-made edges and as wide as two city blocks, loomed up before me like a dark finger beckoning me to it. Walking toward the edge I saw that it had been cut straight down with a piece of heavy equipment; it looked far deeper than I was tall.

Hands in my coat pockets, I stepped closer to the edge. My overheated body would enjoy the coolness of the dark, deep water—a black nothing mirroring how I felt. I walked to within a few feet of the edge. I didn't see any stones near the surface, just black water, a deep abyss. I took another step. The Citadel bells tolled and I counted them. Midnight. I took another step and looked into the water. It wouldn't be bad. Just a deep breath and I wouldn't hurt anymore. Who would know? Who would care? Certainly no one here. The anger within me eased off, the internal fire dying to embers. I felt calm when the decision was made. I knew this had been there, at the edge of my consciousness for quite a while.

Then I heard something. Turning around, I saw nothing. Maybe someone will do the job for me. Stab me and leave me to die—hope it won't last long, dying, that is.

There it was again, a faint sound. A voice? Looking back to the water, I took another step, to the very edge, the front of my military shoes hanging over. Another few inches and I would stop hurting.

I heard it again. I tilted my head slightly to better hear. It came in a very soft whisper "Family." I knew I was alone, yet it came louder a third time "Family."

My brain brought up the images of my brothers and sisters and I felt guilty that I hadn't thought of them in so long. Only one word, but it was enough. I turned and walked to the phone booth on the corner, wondering who or what had spoken.

"…yes, Mom, I promise to stay home. Just wire the money first thing in the morning." Hanging up, I felt drained of what little energy I had left and seriously wondered if I had the strength to make the two blocks back to my apartment.

The next morning the wired money arrived, and I called Jonnie and asked her to come over that afternoon. She arrived at the apartment with a different man and glanced at all the open suitcases and my closed footlocker.

Before she could say anything, I asked "Jonnie, will you take my footlocker back with you and send it to this address for me? I'm leaving tonight to go home and the bus company won't allow me to take the trunk with me."

She looked relieved and I didn't understand why. "Sure," she responded. She nodded to the man. He picked up the trunk, hefted it onto his shoulders, and walked outside to a station wagon. Jonnie, following close behind him, chirped, "I'll send it next week, giving you time to get home." A strained silence rose between us when she added, "Lady, I hope you find happiness when you get there. You know, you've changed a lot since you transferred here."

She gave me a quick hug and was gone before what she had

said registered. It was curious, because I thought she was the one who had changed.

While I finished my packing, my mind was busy with thoughts of home. Remembering that tiny front yard, now seeded with grass, and the painted front porch, lifted my spirits more than a little. The one thing I thought stole my life in my youth was now injecting life into my soul—family.

The cab driver carried my suitcases to the idling bus for me. I tipped him, feeling generous for the first time in a very long time. I got on the Greyhound, sat next to the window, and waited. My life was turning again, but there was no excitement this time. There was nothing but relief. Lost in thought, I felt the bus moving and realized we were backing out of the terminal. Driving past familiar landmarks in the town that had given me so much grief, including the restaurant, I was surprised to feel a deep, fathomless sorrow.

My depression, pushed down and suppressed during the arrangements of going home, now returned. I had failed, again. I was going home without having succeeded at anything. I was going home with my tail between my legs after asking my mother for help. Knowing how little money she had, I hadn't dared ask for the rent money owed the landlord. But I was okay with that. Let him lose as I had lost.

The scenery speeding past the windows reminded me of my life, blurred and surreal; the tires humming on the road, eating up the miles beneath them, gave me the sensation that my life was speeding out of control.

I immediately straightened my back, "Enough. No more."

Strong resolve welled up from the depths of my being. Outside the window, the trees and hills tumbling by, I was reminded again of my life tumbling head over heels. And I hardened myself against it.

No more will I be used. No more, will I allow another to use me. No one will ever force me down to the depths of despair again. This time, I shall stand alone and not rely on any one…for anything.

Snowdrop—
Hope, consolation

During the fourteen-hour bus ride, I slept on and off, talked with other passengers, and got off the bus to stretch my legs when I could. During the quiet hours, I thought of my time spent in the Navy and wondered what had gone wrong. I had spent a long time putting my deep, dark anger in its place, a place so dark I wouldn't have to think about it or look at it ever again.

The rising sun showed me the same dawn I had experienced sixteen months earlier on that first train ride to boot camp. Another house appeared on the horizon. But this one showed more than a single light in one room; the whole house was lit up. It was as though someone had woken to an alarm, or was afraid of the dark and had turned on every light for company and comfort. A small red flag went up inside me and I pushed it down. I was tired of red flags. I just wanted to close my eyes and not open them up until I had reached a better place, a place where I didn't hurt.

After phoning a cab, I sat down on a bench outside the bus terminal and waited. Looking around, I realized things looked different. I didn't recall the town looking so dirty with trash in the streets and gutters; old buildings needed of repair or paint. Then my senses went numb, and my mind drifted off into nothingness. I don't know how long I had been daydreaming when the cab appeared out of thin air. Even the ride home was surreal. I recognized all the houses and the street signs, but they didn't feel familiar.

Mom helped me with my suitcases, not saying much except to ask how I was doing. Not encouraging conversation, I replied, "Fine," in a flat voice.

Walking into my old bedroom, shared with five sisters, who were all in school that day, I noticed someone had taken my things out of the dresser and taped them onto the mirror. Angry, I yanked them off and threw them into the bathroom wastebasket. They were things belonging to a child I no longer knew or even recognized. I didn't feel like an adult, either. How is an adult supposed to feel? Worldly? Wise?

My mother had made arrangements for a visit to Aunt Helen, and I was surprised when, having learned how to drive, she drove me there herself. Feeling better with cool air rushing past my face from the open window, I teased her about my needing glasses because of the blurred scenery speeding by so fast. I exchanged smiled and hugs with my cousins while Aunt Helen was on the phone. Upon hanging up, she turned on the TV.

A newsman spoke in a loud voice while film footage showed President Kennedy being fatally shot and falling into Jackie's arms.

The scenario had taken place two hours earlier, and all the stations were running the footage on a loop. When the newsman said all transportation in the country would halt the following Monday in honor of President John F. Kennedy's death, my only thoughts were that President Kennedy was in a good place, and I was glad I had taken the bus this Friday. Mildly surprised at my insensitivity, I thought no more about it. The TV was turned off and we played catch-up in between my aunt's shocked concerns regarding the president and the world at large.

My reunion with my brothers and sisters later that day was exciting…for them. They seemed younger than I remembered. After a very short while they went their separate directions, leaving me alone, but not without glancing back with questioning looks. I was sure they, too, were wondering at the changes in me and I was curious about what they saw.

Walking in a fog most of the time, I searched for a job. I applied for a job as a receptionist at Ma Bell. The man there told me to come back in two weeks; he told me this twice. A month later, he told me for the third time to come back. I asked him what his game was.

"Oh, nothing. I heard about you WAVES and I just wanted to see if you were as dumb as I was told. Guess the guys were right."

His hands were dangling over the front of his chair's arm rests while he was laughing. I leaned over the table and pushed fast and hard with my strong legs. When I slammed the door, he was still cussing and rubbing his hands. The whole Navy thing had been a waste of time, so I stopped using it as a reference.

I worked as a waitress at a couple of restaurants, trying to find some way to financially make my way out of the house. I tried working both jobs at the same time. After two weeks, I didn't make it to either. When I gave my notice the next day at the A&W, the owner's wife accused me of leaving because I couldn't have her husband, whom I rarely saw and didn't like.

Her accusation brought back Navy memories I thought I had buried in the recesses of my mind. My skewed sleep patterns returned. I'd go to sleep, wake up with a very active brain, stare at the ceiling, go back to sleep, and wake up tired. A few days later, I had a blackout. When I came to, I behaved like a stranger and didn't know anyone. Scared, Mom talked me back to bed for a nap. Three hours later I was fine. It was my turn to be scared; scared I was losing my mind because I couldn't remember the incident at all.

I found a job in a bowling alley that was also a restaurant and lounge. I enjoyed this job and became good at cooking, waiting on tables, and bartending. It not only kept me busy and my mind occupied, working hard also tuned out the world. Staying focused, my efficiency increased and expanded my multitasking abilities. My employer praised my work, often, and the more I was praised, the harder I worked. Within a few months, I was the head waitress and got the coveted 2-10 p.m. shift during the week and the 12-6 p.m. shift on Sundays. This gave me the time to sleep normal hours—when I wasn't hitting the other bars and lounges.

My depression went away. Feeling good again, my sex drive increased tremendously, and within two months of one of my short affairs, I became pregnant. When I approached the baby's father about marriage, his response was to marry the "town whore," instead of me. Angry, I filed a paternity lawsuit. He was jailed, and I gained a reputation as "the bitch."

I believed the child I carried was mine to love and, with care, I would teach the child to love me back. I related this to my pregnant mother, who was positive she was carrying a boy, and she spoke of her raising my child with my brother. I knew she was trying to rescue me and my "reputation" because she had been shunned by society after giving birth to me, but I would have none of it.

Mom gave birth to her tenth child in November. The following January, after having felt life for a month, I miscarried my first child, also a son. The pregnancy left a different kind of hole. I couldn't say the hole was in my heart because I wasn't sure I had one. The hole had found another space to occupy in my body, enlarging the already present void. I was also surprised such emptiness could ache so much. As time passed the hole didn't shrink, I just felt it less and less.

Two months later, I met my future husband, Jim. He was good-looking, had nice manners and an easy laugh. Testing him, I took my brother along on our first date. Jim sat him between us in the show and interacted with him throughout the evening. I didn't feel he was a threat to me. Indeed, he did everything he could to please me. When the expected rejection didn't come, I began to wonder about the money he spent on me and whether he could support me on his delivery job.

Though we barely spoke of marriage, three weeks from the day of our first date, we went into a jewelers, and he bought the ring set I had already picked out a few days earlier. On April Fool's Day, I officially received my engagement ring. A week later, he actually proposed marriage. I don't know if I told him I loved him. I just wanted a way out of the house and someone to care for me.

After starting a new state job two-and-a-half hours away, Jim came into the lounge after closing time and asked if we could elope. Wiping down booths, I said, "Sure, I'll go get a veil to match my white uniform, pick up some flowers and—" Standing upright, I saw the expression on Jim's face. "You're serious," I said, stunned.

Before he got his new job, we had planned a July church wedding for the sake of his Italian, Roman Catholic family. But working out of town, it occurred to him I might find someone else in his absence. We were married on June 1st, a Tuesday night, by a Justice of the Peace, with my mother and stepfather as witnesses.

During the two-hour drive to our apartment, I thought it was a good time to ask Jim how much money he had. He asked, "How much was your check today?"

"It was $80." I responded, red flags going up again. "Why?"

Turning toward me and smiling, he replied "We have $80."

I couldn't believe my ears. "What were you taking me out on all this time? Where did the money come from for the apartment and the groceries?"

"While you were working I was playing poker. My winnings paid for our dates. As for the apartment, that came from my savings which are now zero." He was still smiling, proud of himself.

Technically, I had been duped again, with no immediate way out of this one. *Curious! This time I actually don't feel trapped.*

Monkshood—Beware

Our three-room apartment was the front half of the second floor of a large Victorian house in a neighborhood fast becoming seedy. Cooking and cleaning for two people didn't take up much time, so I found a job. Clerking at a paper company, I learned in a hurry I didn't care for such a strict schedule: rising, fixing breakfast, going to work for a short time, break, work, lunch, work, break, work, home for supper then bed again. If a thing became rote, I wanted to leave it behind and go on to something else.

Six months after our elopement, I became pregnant. With Jim being Italian and the oldest, his family took the news of my pregnancy in the grand style of Italians who knew how to celebrate. There were meetings with relatives, talk of baby names, showers to be given, and invitations to be sent. The list was endless, and I soon noticed that my family was scarcely mentioned. Thus, a small rift between our two families began; yet the whole thing remained a wonder to me. My experience was: Mom got pregnant, gave birth, and then brought the baby home—without any of the fanfare I was experiencing.

The celebration was short-lived, however. I miscarried my second baby, my husband's first. For me, there were no tears this time. Not only did losing the baby anger me, my husband angered me more for putting me in a position of experiencing another loss. My relationship with his family changed. I had failed again, failed everyone. Jim and I never discussed the miscarriage. Perhaps we should have. But our life got busy again and I went back to work.

During the next year, Jim kept track of the bills, and we both discovered I could spend more than we made. Even if I used my own paycheck just for me, it wasn't enough to pay for the stuff I *had* to have. My spending habits created arguments that never dented my spending. If anything, it got worse. We attended a lot of parties, weddings, and holidays, and sometimes we gave parties. At any event serving alcohol, I usually ended up partially or totally drunk.

In the fall after our second anniversary, I became pregnant again, only to lose it three months later. We didn't discuss this loss either. Within a short time I started picking on Jim for little things and not always the same things. He responded by bowling more nights a week, or golfing, and spending time golfing with his coworkers on the weekend.

By this time, we had moved into a mobile home in a small mobile-home park and were meeting people outside his job. My maternal needs strong, I started babysitting again. I watched a five-month-old infant until she turned two. Her mother decided I had too much contact and severed the relationship when her daughter kept asking for me on the weekends. I wanted very much to stay home, but learned I wasn't happy there either. Always needing something to occupy my time, hands, and brain, I entered the workforce again.

I went from job to job, a clerk for one place, a receptionist at another, and then I became a key-tape operator and instructor for the federal government. Depression set in again. Sometimes, I'd sleep after coming home from work, wake up, then go back to bed around eleven and sleep through the night. Then there were nights I didn't sleep at all and sat up watching TV or doing needle work, which I usually gave away.

My father-in-law had passed away a couple years before. My mother-n-law, having problems with her son Tim, had asked if we would take him. So Tim moved in to stay with us soon after my sister arrived. She also came to live with us because I could help her get a mini-degree in Data Keypunch and teach her as well. After she left, we learned how badly she had treated him when we weren't around—and us, by lying to the neighbors. Tim moved with us to a newly built apartment complex and never gave us a problem. He made good grades and surprised everyone, including his Mother, by being affectionate with family members whenever we went home for a visit. Watching him grow into a loving person gratified my maternal instincts, even though it was surrogate.

We were in the apartment only a few months when my mother-in-law started pestering us to let Tim come back home. He was doing so well and I knew if he lived with his mother, he would fall back in with his old friends and revert back to his old habits. Soon,

Tim added his voice, then my husband joined in—three people doing a nagging song and dance on me. I couldn't fight all three, so I acquiesced. When summer came, my husband and I were by ourselves again.

Mom and I made a major leap in our relationship, each forgiving the other. On one of our visits home, my mother and I went shopping and stopped at our favorite hot dog place, where the recipe was still a family secret. Her tab was only a dollar tab. I thought back to when I was thirteen and had wanted to see *South Pacific* for the sixth time because it had been such a wonderful escape for me. When I asked for a dollar to go to the show, Mom told me she had only two dollars. The argument got so heated I slapped her. Shocked, we stood frozen, staring at each other. Shame forced me to bolt upstairs to my room where I threw myself on my bed and cried. After a few moments Mom came upstairs, quietly slipped into the room, and laid a dollar on the bed. Still angry, I said, "I don't want it." She said nothing as she slipped softly out of the room.

I went to the show. But every time after the incident, when I tried to give her back the dollar, she refused, making me hurt again. When our order came, I looked at Mom.

She looked out the car windshield. Having gone through this scenario a few times before, she understood the silence. She sat quietly for a moment before turning toward me, smiling. "It's time."

I knew I would do well with children, but I never allowed myself to think about it as I lost babies three, four, and five.

Kelly Girls was an ideal employer, and I stayed with them off and on for several years, in between other jobs. I worked when I wanted, and never at the same job. But when a position opened up in the city hall's data processing department, I was hired based on my work as a temporary Kelly Girl several weeks before in the same position. It wasn't until I became their computer operator did it occur to me I was rectifying my failure in not graduating from data processing in the Navy.

With a city employee's salary coming in, Jim and I climbed the financial ladder and broadened our circle of friends as our social status rose. We were surprised at the caliber of people we met in what society labeled Middle America. I didn't know what to expect but it wasn't the greed or the depth of the "me" attitude.

Near our tenth anniversary, I became pregnant for the sixth time.

✻

Dark CrimsonRose—Mourning

In my fifth month with life stirring within me, I quit my job. We bought another mobile home and moved out into the country. I fell in love with country life, and within a month, I knew we would never live in the city again. Memories of my childhood came back to me as I planted a vegetable garden on the edge of an open field and looked forward to canning our own food. I had always made our bread.

Gardening and settling into mobile-home park living, I allowed myself to think about this baby as a person and dared to buy a few pieces of clothes, knowing the rest would be hand-me-downs. I was sure I'd be content as a stay-at-home Mom, putting up my home-grown produce, and filling the freezer for the winter, and planning for our child.

In my sixth month, one month after experiencing my unborn son's kicks, I felt the all-too-familiar pains. I called Jim at work, and waited the ten minutes for him to come home. Time stood still long enough for me to regress into a numbed robot. It must have been long enough for Jim, as well, for neither of us spoke as we drove to the hospital. In the ER, I went through the ritual of discerning whether or not I was having false labor. A nurse, me in my wheelchair, and Jim, holding my suitcase, went up in elevator to the third floor. It moved in slow motion, prolonging the inevitable. The air inside thickened as the silence grew heavier, smothering us as we ascended. With crystal clarity, I heard the gears humming, clicking, echoing, resonating in the silence and dancing off the walls of the elevator.

Mutely, we put my clothes in the closet as I slipped on the familiar gown I had worn several times before. When I got into bed and was waiting for the nurse to come back for my vitals, I looked at Jim and said, "You may as well go home. There's nothing more you can do here." He nodded his head solemnly and bent down to kiss my cheek. I couldn't look at him.

I had failed. Again. My body had rejected me. Again.

✻

After midnight my labor intensified, and I was taken to a prep room. Since it wasn't a birthing room, I knew my baby wasn't expected to survive. My blood pressure rose to 200 over 150, so I was given an injection to bring it down and knock me out. Through all of this, I had not said a word, not even a moan during the contractions; the robot had taken over my senses.

While the doctor stood in the corner, waiting for the medication to kick in, she told a nurse, "If she gets pregnant again, it may kill her." At this point the nurse standing at my side tried frantically to get the doctor's attention, to let her know I was still awake and able to hear what was being said. Thirty minutes later the doctor stood over me and informed me she was going to have to "take" the baby. I nodded as two nurses, one on each of my knees, pressed down and held my knees apart as the next contraction came. I was nearly unconsciousness when the doctor reached into my body and grabbed the baby's head. As she pulled I felt my stomach muscles resisting. At the moment I gave up all hope, my body released my baby.

She deftly pulled him out and wrapped him up. I couldn't see him before she cut the umbilical cord. After it was over, I was cleansed and moved me into my room. A pair of scissors, still attached to the umbilical cord, was placed on my stomach, should the after-birth come on its own. When it didn't, a nurse came and pushed on my abdomen with the pressure like a steamroller. It was like giving birth all over again. She pulled on the umbilical cord until I felt the afterbirth come loose from inside. Again, I made no sound. Thirty minutes later the doctor came in and asked again if I wanted her to call Jim. I said no. I later learned he cried in the middle of the night, from a sense of knowing. I also learned after a couple of weeks that the baby and the afterbirth somehow got lost on their way to the pathologist, so I never learned why I miscarried.

A couple months after my miscarriage, my parents came to visit. Mom wanted to make sure I was okay. Jim's mother and grand-mother came a few days later, but their visit made me feel worse. My brother-in-law, Tim, wanted to come back to live with us again. It hadn't been long before his old problems resurfaced after he moved back home. When my mother-in-law asked if she could "give him back to us," I told her we had to talk first.

It angered me that she could bounce her child back and forth like this, taking her son's emotions—and ours—in the same directions. I wanted to force her to take responsibility for her child and not allow her to just toss him out like a bag of garbage. Jim reminded me how hard it had been for her since his father died.

I told her we'd need compensation for her son to live with us because we couldn't support a teenager on Jim's salary. Her response was, "Oh, I couldn't let go of his check. I need a new car."

I didn't expect such coldness from her and thought it was an incredibly cruel remark to make in front of her own child. I responded by closing my gaping mouth, looking at Tim, and saying, "You know where you stand now, don't you?"

He bowed his head. I wasn't sure if he was sad because of what his mother had just said or because he couldn't come back *home* to us.

Several months after the miscarriage, after all the visits from well-wishers, after all the hours of stirring juices and jams, after picking, snapping, and washing everything I had canned for the winter, after watching and listening to the leaves fall, and after talking it over with Jim, I had surgical sterilization. Hearing the doctor say I would die if I tried another pregnancy, I felt my life still had worth and decided not to sacrifice it. And I didn't want to go through having another life torn out of my body because I couldn't support or nurture one. The following spring, instead of looking forward to birth, I was sterilized beyond reparation. Leaving the hospital, I felt an odd sense of freedom. I no longer had to worry about killing another baby or failing people.

Striped Carnation—A love cannot be

Having learned the GI Bill would pay me a monthly allotment, I went to school full time in the secretarial field. College was a boost to my ego as I discovered my many abilities, not only in the office, but in golf, self-defense, and art. I explored a whole new world I had been too busy in the past to study—and that new world was me. My creative writing instructor introduced me to Shakespeare and literature became a joy. I still didn't care for math, but I enjoyed the Math of Finance course, where I learned to calculate interest rates and mortgages. My own diversity was the biggest discovery of all. I could do whatever I wanted as long as I didn't listen to other people telling me I couldn't.

I found it interesting that off-campus people were the ones limiting my boundaries. I looked around at those who were educated and those who were not and realized how an individual's openness usually depended on how much awareness they had, and whether it was schooled or self-taught. Discovering my openness, my curiosity and appetite for knowledge grew ferociously and in many directions. Before completing my studies for an associate degree in applied science, I received an associate degree in liberal arts.

Thinking enough time had passed and I had healed from the loss of my last baby, I approached Jim about adoption. I knew he was doing it more for me than for himself when he didn't take much convincing. After much research, we ended up at a state agency and, instead of an infant, adopted a nine-year-old. Even state agencies lie. We were told they had processed Brian through their system, but we learned he hadn't been at the agency two months when we came along. All the while Jim kept asking me if it was what I wanted to do, but I had turned off red flags a long time ago.

Even with Brian's behavior and emotional problems, and his seeing a psychiatrist, we tried to adopt him a year later. By then the agency had lost us in the system and didn't know who we were. When they found us in the system a week later, we filed the papers and adopted Brian anyway. The next spring, Jim transferred upstate.

During the year Jim was upstate, personal items belonging to me disappeared only to reappear in the same place hours later. It never happened when Jim was home, only when he was away. Food went missing, and Brian denied taking it. It was only after I found maggots shriveling on the kitchen floor that I found food under the cabinets. Searching his room, I found other missing items hidden under our son's mattress. Brian had brought with him a bed wetting problem. We had worked with the psychiatrist on the issue and thought we had made progress.

On one particularly cold morning, I found Brian's wet pajamas frozen between the wall and his bed, after months and months of working with him. Standing there, holding his wet pajamas, rage welled up and filled my chest with strength I doubted myself capable of feeling. I backhanded the dresser, which stood on high-pile carpet, hard enough to shove it against the wall. If I had hit Brian, he would have been seriously injured. I had managed to bury my anger for several years, and to live what I felt was a normal life, but, this sudden, intense rage frightened me.

Jim was home for Christmas, and things were fine. Three days after Jim went back upstate, I was hospitalized for three days after the New Year's holiday. He had to come back home again. My doctor said I should get rid of Brian, that If I didn't, within a few short months of holding down two jobs, going to school full time, and traveling between three different cities, I'd be in an insane asylum.

I didn't listen.

Things went well for about two months before items began to show up missing again. My lipstick disappeared off the kitchen table only to reappear a couple of hours later. Food items vanished, and I couldn't find them this time. I questioned my sanity. I sensed Jim found it hard to believe everything I told him because things were normal to him, when he was home on the weekends. There was no way to convince him because I knew Brian would deny everything. It angered me that I had to defend myself at all. I kept quiet.

One morning, I was worn out from the extra load of homework I had finished the night before. I went to my purse for my comb and discovered it gone. I stood there for a few moments trying to remember when I had last used it, but I couldn't think straight. I knew I kept a comb in my purse; and my favorite pen was also missing. I kept my purse in my bedroom closet. There was no way anyone could have taken it without my knowing, and there was no way I could have lost those items…or was there? Right then, I truly questioned my sanity. Perhaps my doctor was right. Perhaps I was slowly losing my mind and I was in denial. I didn't want to admit defeat, but I didn't want to admit a child could best me, either. Feeling helpless, I picked up the phone to call my doctor for the name of a psychiatrist. I looked up at the clock to see if she would be in her…

"It's gone," I whispered, staring at the empty space on the dining room wall where the clock should have been. I was shocked. But I also knew I was okay, my sanity was intact. The missing clock was proof. That clock was the one thing in our house that was never moved, never touched. I immediately went into Brian's bedroom. I had always contended that one's bedroom was their sanctuary, not to be invaded without the occupant's permission. That morning I was going to do more than invade it.

I went through Brian's drawers and cried when I found my personal items, missing for several months and forgotten. I continued through his closet and found more items I knew didn't belong to Brian, to any of us. When I lifted the mattress I found the missing clock. The casing had been removed and the internal parts sticking up had made a hole through the wet mattress, causing the metal parts to rust. *When could he have taken the clock?* Brian had been hiding his bed wetting again. I hesitated before looking behind the bed for fear of what I would find. Finally, moving the bed, I found two pairs of wet pajamas frozen to the wall and covered with black mold. The tape-stripping sound created when I pulled them away from the wall was the same sound I *felt,* as though something was also silently being stripped away from my heart.

I remembered the promise I'd made to myself on the bus returning home from the Navy. My robotic sense returned as I went back to the kitchen and called the caseworker. Things blurred after that. The caseworker came…she explained they had funds to help us…it's too late…can we talk…I've told you all…the call from Brian, crying and saying he was sorry…going to court to rescind the adoption…instructors allowing me to leave college early…neighbors not talking…friends not coming around…everyone blaming us…packing up our mobile home….

Jim was behind the wheel of our car, following the mobile home in front of us when my mind slowly registered my present reality and I came back from wherever I had been. We were on our way to a new place.

We talked about everything. He didn't blame me. Indeed, he felt it was his fault because he wasn't there to share the burden. It occurred to me then that I hadn't really shared everything with him. I dealt with the situation as I had always dealt with any problems. I handled them alone.

As we pulled out onto the highway, I kept my gaze forward, I didn't look back. But the mind plays tricks. As the car moved out of the mobile home park, built in the middle of a corn field, my mind dredged up memories of Brian playing with the park owner's son. I remembered the owner driving the tractor with the disc harrow, and his son, standing next to his father, falling backwards off the tractor and into the moving discs. Death was instantaneous. My mind stretched farther back, like a hand reaching into a dark abyss, and grasped pictures of nurses holding my swaddled dead babies. Straightening my back and flexing my shoulders, I closed my eyes and turned inward. During the 240-mile north, I slowly, methodically erased all I could—about Brian, about the miscarriages, about my failures, about…everything.

*

Scarlet Poppy—Fantastic

The move became a new start for us. Jim enjoyed his new work environment and his coworkers, and he became good friends with his boss. I found a secretarial position in the engineering department of a paper company. Less than a year later I went to work for the county's probate court. This job intrigued me. Clerk to the court and probate judge, assistant to the administrator, certified court recorder for the juvenile hearings, and secretary to the juvenile officer (JO) were among my main duties. The clerk's job allowed me access into the workings of the police station. My correspondence skills afforded me the opportunity to contact other county court clerks for adjudications of juveniles who had received traffic violations from the state police. There was just one glitch on this job. The judge acted too much like a father.

In the past, once I learned a job, I became efficient enough to be left alone. When I left a position, two or three people were needed to replace me. This judge liked to keep his hand in in the offices for which he was responsible, and this meant supervising me. And this did not sit well. Added to this tight rein, were my weekly visits to his chambers for reprimands for what he felt were social misconducts. Smiling, he'd say things like, "We do not call the commissioners 'turkeys.' When you step out of this office, you represent this court…." This went on for about six months until one day I went into his office and performed my weekly ritual of closing the door, turning around, and plopping into his leather visitor's chair, making it go "whoosh."

The judge simply handed me a piece of paper and said, "I need three copies."

Expecting another reproof for something I had done or said in public, I was totally caught off guard. I stared at him in disbelief. "Is that all? The copier is right outside the door."

"I know where it is." He had been smiling from the time I had come in.

I made the copies, walked into his office, and put the papers on his desk. "Is that it?" I asked with my hands on my hips, again waiting for the other shoe to drop.

"Yes. Thank you," he responded, still smiling.

He picked up a sheet of paper and started reading, my signal to leave. I floated down the hall to my office. On some level, it felt good to have a man of his caliber possibly approving me, and my behavior. This was something I had expected from my father but never got. Yet at the same time, I was angry and agitated and couldn't understand why. My mood continued for a couple of days, making the JO ask what was up. I didn't know and said as much. But I could relate the change to that particular visit to the judge's office. She suggested I talk to the psychiatrist who sat in on the Monday meetings with social workers and professionals representing the county agencies and schools. She called and I went in the next day. I thought he couldn't be very good if I could get in right away. I later learned he had used his lunch hour.

Sitting in his office, I rattled off what I thought was jumbled sentences. And I was amazed at what came out of my mouth and how fast—similar to opening the barn door and all the excited horses stampeding out. After forty-five minutes, he gently raised his hand and went to the blackboard. He explained how people are three things: a child, a parent, and an adult. I had always been the parent and the adult but never the child. The judge evoked the child within me by closely supervising my job performance and correcting my behaviors, things my father had never done. Since I wasn't comfortable as the child, I became agitated. The good doctor also suggested I do one thing, a thing I vowed I would never do: He suggested I go home and ask my husband to take care of me.

"Now, why in the hell would I do a thing like that?" I asked, suddenly not liking this man.

Returning to his seat, he said, "You need to take care of your inner child. Nurture her."

"I'm an adult, not a child," I barked, irritated because I had to remind him.

"We need to nurture the child within us so we don't lose the ability to play. The adult has the role of being responsible in our society and in the workplace. The parent has the role of nurturing and teaching family members and creating a home." He rose from his chair while saying gently, "You think about it. If you need to talk more, call me."

After talking with the JO about the session with the doctor, I was quiet the rest of the day, thinking about what he had said. It appeared that, as a child, I behaved as the adult and the parent when I thought I had been playing. I had never actually *played*. Though, in retrospect, I remembered sitting in the living room playing with my dolls when I told Mom, "Daddy's dead." I couldn't remember when I had *played* after that. I sat at my desk for a very long time wondering why I had stopped. Just thinking of asking my husband to take care of me created a hundred butterflies, fluttering like crazy inside my stomach. Despite what I had said to the doctor, it had never occurred to me *not* to do what he suggested because I wanted to learn to play. I badly wanted to learn *how* to play.

Later that evening I called Jim into the bedroom and we sat on the bed as I tried several times to ask the question. I made no correlation between the bed and the question, "Would you take care of me?" For some reason it had to be on the bed, not in the living room or in the dining room. Jim got irritable after he came into the bedroom four times and I still couldn't say it. Three days later, I finally blurted it out.

Confused, he responded, "I thought I was." When I didn't say anything more, he got off the bed and asked, "Is that all?" He didn't understand and I didn't have the words to explain it to him. I didn't know how to tell him I needed to play and I was asking him to teach me. During my silence he left the room. We never discussed it again.

While I worked in the court, the JO tried her best to talk me into fostering children. She had watched how I related with the kids when they came into the office. I explained it was because I wasn't an authority figure, therefore, not threatening. I was simply the mother who listened. It didn't take too much convincing, though, because before long Jim and I became foster parents for children fifteen or older. I stipulated wanting children needing long-term placements, not sleepovers. Within a week we had a sixteen year old, one month into the tenth grade.

I took to Phil immediately. He was a dark, moody teenager with a quiet demeanor. When he went out, which was often, he was either walking or hanging out with a male friend and the friend's sister. His need to keep moving constantly should have triggered a lot of familiar red flags for me. We tried to create a family environment with a teenager who said he wanted it, but never stayed home long enough to be a part of it. We went through a lot of traumas with him, from alcohol abuse to a suicide attempt. But we wouldn't let go; I couldn't let go.

Toward the end of the school year, after learning of Phil's truancy, I discussed our problems with the JO. The following week, she and I attended the Monday meeting of professionals, including the same psychiatrist with whom I'd had my one meeting. After I related our problems, several of the twenty attendees made suggestions. When we all fell silent, everyone turned their heads in unison and looked to the good doctor. He suggested a contract between

Phil, me and Jim, and to not move Phil to another foster home, as someone had suggested. I had argued that point; moving him to another foster home would only move the problem, not solve it.

That night, I told Jim what took place at the meeting, how frustrated I felt at not knowing what else to do, and how I had argued to keep Phil from being moved. I was startled into silence when I heard a step, and then Phil's door closed quietly. I thought he was out; he was never home at dinnertime. I had always been up front with Phil about what I was going to do about anything pertaining to him before I did it, except this time. I'd like to think that hearing me tell Jim about fighting for him to stay with us, while I cried, was the reason Phil gave us no further problems. We grew closer and started doing things together as a family; but we were not as close as I would have liked a son to be. He still spent a great deal of his time with his friend. Over the next two years his grades came up, but rarely above a C. After graduating high school he joined the Navy.

By the following spring we had moved to a rural village in a neighboring county, closer to where Jim worked, and we bought our first house. Six months later, before Thanksgiving, we contacted the judge to file an Order of Entry since Phil used to be a ward of his court. Jim and I had discussed adopting Phil, but we wanted to give him time. We thought eighteen months away from us, his natural mother and stepfather, and his friends would be long enough.

After picking Phil up at the airport, I sensed something in his silence and gave him time and space. It was the same distancing of himself I had sensed in a few of his letters and some of his collect phone calls. Nervous, I hoped the right time would avail itself to ask if he wanted to be adopted, preferably before the Monday appointment. Jim had thought it lunacy to make the appointment when we hadn't yet discussed it with Phil, yet.

While I was cooking his favorite dinner, Phil paced the kitchen and around the table like all the kids did when something was bothering them. Suddenly, he blurted, "Mom, why don't you and Dad adopt me?"

I stared at him, raised a finger to signal I needed a moment, and went into the bedroom to compose myself. I couldn't cry, but I couldn't speak either. I was so elated. Walking back into the kitchen, I calmly replied, "We have an appointment on Monday to go before the judge." Jim heard the conversation from the living room. At the dinner table we were all quiet—the sort of quiet containing a sense of peace that usually comes after a long, hard struggle.

On Monday, after the court hearing, Phil disappeared without telling us where he was going and I was upset when he came back. Right in the middle of my telling him we had an appointment with a photographer, he brought out two boxes from behind his back and handed one to each of us. In the two boxes were two mugs, one said MOM and the other said DAD. In that moment, I again realized I couldn't cry, and I didn't know when I had lost the ability. I vividly remember knowing the pain in my chest would not have been as great had I been able to shed the tears of joy I felt. All I could do was smile.

✳

Forget-me-not

After a year at the court, I went to work for a state institution as an accountant. I stayed on that job for a year before transferring to another state job near Jim's workplace as secretary to an office of CPAs. Most of the men in the office smoked, with two enjoying cigars. Within a year, I developed an allergy to tobacco smoke that forced me to quit. Another reason for moving closer to Jim's work had been our new home in the country, located outside the city limits of where Jim worked.

In this house, we had six more foster children. They taught me a great deal about parenting while I grew as an adult. I drew a hard line and was a tough parent, but it was okay because the kids also knew they were loved. They could count on me to be honest with them, sometimes painfully so. I did my best to teach them to have and maintain integrity with and in all things. Each child knew what we expected of him or her, and they knew what they could expect from us. This knowledge allowed them a large arena in which they were comfortable enough to explore themselves.

Through the teenagers and their families, I learned quite a few lessons in human behavior and psychological patterns. After finding their niche in our family and settling into school, which usually took about six weeks, the foster kids had their first contact with their own families. By this time they were relaxed and were able to listen or talk with their family members and with their case workers.

Since the age of twenty-one, I had been approached by people who wanted counseling. In the beginning I had just listened. Through the years I began to do more than listen, and discovered I had an innate ability to look into a person or a situation and bring to the surface what needed to be discussed.

I began to notice a pattern in human behavior coinciding with certain forms of abuse. Our teenage foster children honed my observation skills. With each teenager, their family members were surprised at how much the child had changed when they came in contact with them again. It fascinated me to watch everyone in their human dances. But it also saddened me to see they were unaware that love was the music and the reason. Somewhere along the way I found myself loving people, never understanding from where it came. I wondered if, on one level, I smiled and loved so no one could see the internal me. On another level I wondered if I gave what I had not received in my youth, if so, where did I learn it?

We kept our license for seven years. It was after that I built my herb business. There was no cure for my allergy to tobacco smoke, but a magazine I had read in a doctor's office said goldenseal root was good for sinuses, my main problem. Usually, it took a bulldozer to get me to move or act, but this tiny bit of information spurred me on to build a small herb garden. Jim said it was okay, but before I could dig it up, I had heavy equipment cleaning out the scrub pine and brush in front of our property where we created over 7,500 square feet of raised-bed gardens with the help of a sixteen-year-old workaholic.

Before the summer was over, that same bulldozer leveled off the same amount of area in back of the house for a greenhouse, a six-foot pond, experimental beds, and cold frames. It didn't take six months for me to go from a pain in the nose to building my own business. And did I have ideas!

Creating exhilarated me. I was not a failure. I lived and breathed the business as I designed and built the cabinets that held the dry goods, I built a spice rack that held 252 different kinds of bulk herbs, and built and stained counters to contrast with the herbal products and wreaths I created. I felt alive! I loved kneeling on the ground and digging or planting in the dirt. I loved watching the plants grow from seed to maturity, like watching children grow from the dark womb to adulthood. I never got over the feeling of having done it before with a childlike person, but the memory remained elusive.

We cleaned out the garage and turned it into a store. Later we added a 30' x 40' garage, part of the back half was a store room. The other side of the store room was my workshop full of woodworking stools, and the front half of the building was the two-car garage. A couple years later, we converted the storeroom into a small classroom for workshops. From the first day we opened our doors, we were busy. Within a year people traveled from all over to see the gardens and attend my workshops and lectures. Buying clubs from three states came to purchase our plants. Large corporations approached me about lectures and workshops. My business didn't just grow and succeed; I grew and became successful with it.

My innate abilities were one thing, but a canoe accident brought forth other things. One weekend Jim and I were arguing while paddling on the river. He grabbed onto branches and logs in the river to stop the canoe, and I tried to teach him to backpaddle to stop and maneuver. At one juncture, he grabbed an overhead branch, causing the canoe to tip and dump us into the river. Rather than falling to the side, I slid off the seat as the canoe rolled over and hit me on the head.

I thought I came to the surface, wondering at the brightness of the sun. I saw Jim on shore looking, I later learned, for his glasses. About two hundred feet beyond him stood Granny in her favorite dress—the one she had been buried in eight years before—and she was smiling. Feeling the river's current on my body, I pushed up from the bottom of the river, broke the surface like a bobber, and deeply gulped breaths of air.

Two weeks later, I went out before dawn to our dog's pen to investigate why he was so excited. Jim waited at the door and commented on how shocked he was at my having gone out while it was dark. His observation brought me up short. Until that moment I had been terrorized by the dark, to the point of sitting down immediately when the lights went out and not moving until they came back on. Other, less subtle, changes surfaced.

Anything I planted grew—fast. I heard music when the toilet flushed, no kidding. My peripheral vision sometimes caught a woman dressed in turn-of-the-century clothing walking through the foyer from the kitchen to the store. And the biggest change. I saw other people's faces when I touched objects belonging to them. After people in my workshops made potpourri, I was able to read their potpourri, step into their private lives, and give them readings.

I was never wrong.

I had fun with my new talents and thought everyone had them. One sunny day, I stood outside of a store in a neighboring town waiting for Jim, who was still at the checkout. I spotted an elderly Native American with a wise and chiseled face sitting in a chair that leaned back against the building. His stare made me nervous as he slowly got up and came across the street to me. When he stood two feet away, he extended his hand to me. Feeling relieved and smiling, I obliged by placing mine into his. He closed his eyes and when he opened them, I saw his pupils were enlarged.

"One day, when you totally let go of yourself, you will be a great healer." He let go of my hand, turned, and walked away.

In the second it took for me to look for Jim, for testimony, protection, anything, in case he had witnessed the exchange, the Native American was no where to be seen. The shock had worn off by the time Jim finally came out. I said nothing lest he think I was crazy. At that moment I wasn't sure I wasn't.

Two years after opening the business, Mom and Dad moved in with us. We had bought the property with the idea of them moving in, and our expanding the house when they did. Dad's alcoholism had not only affected his health, but his work performance as well. When he retired at 62, there simply wasn't any money. Mom had to work right up to his retirement date just to make ends meet.

We built an addition onto our house, including a sunroom and a separate bedroom for Mom. I didn't know they hadn't been sleeping together for several years. Before they moved in, we added a very large garage and a workshop with Dad in mind. He and I had often talked about his teaching me some of his woodworking and welding skills. I could've saved myself building the workshop and getting excited. My plans went to the wayside as his drinking took control of his life. The rest of us lived around it and left him to it.

After the greenhouse was built and operating, Mom informed me she would work it. Knowing she had always wanted a greenhouse, I left her to it. Eventually, she also took over the people part of the store and left me the paperwork, lectures, and workshops. I was an excellent basket weaver and loom weaver and I sold some of my art pieces in the store. I taught basket weaving and anything herbal in my workshops; my herbology class students included a doctor and two nurses. We became a good team, Mom and I. Working together also gave us time to get to know one another. I grew to love her as someone who had also been emotionally deprived during her childhood. This gave me a better understanding of how and why she couldn't give to us what she herself had not received or learned.

The customers loved her, and I watched her light up and come alive as I have never seen before. Mom, too, grew as the business grew. Years earlier, she had shared with me that Dad mentally and emotionally abused her. I had seen the signs back then and mentioned it, but she denied it. Now, she finally admitted it. I knew if I went to dad, he would turn on Mom. So I waited.

When I caught Mom watching how Jim and I related, I pointed out that I didn't want certain behaviors from Jim and explained what I did to create the behaviors I wanted. Mom tried a few pointers on Dad. He didn't bite. After visiting my sister for a week, Mom came back to find that Dad had done things for himself. All he wanted throughout his life with Mom was a waitress or a gopher, and I refused to be either. My actions taught Mom that she didn't need to cater to him anymore.

So, for a few months before he died, Dad hated me and blamed me because no one catered to his whims. What surprised me was that it didn't bother me. His hard looks told me how he felt, but I couldn't feel anything for him. I didn't even cry when he died. I did, however, clean the house from top to bottom in less than ten hours. He was the first person to die in our immediate family, and cleaning the house was my way of coping. When I remembered not feeling anything, I wondered anew, for a blink of an eye, if something was wrong with me.

When Mom took over more of the business, I attended college to finish my bachelor's degree. I still did workshops, but gave fewer lectures, and she took over the inventory. That summer was the most euphoric time of my life. I lost a tremendous amount of weight and actually enjoyed lovemaking. Jim rose to the occasion admirably. My journeys to one university class and two local community college classes covered a thousand miles of roads. And I loved the freedom of every minute of it.

We were content until after we closed the store in the fall for the season. I noticed Mom had been frequently massaging her legs and was having difficulty walking. We were able to get her a walker. By the end of April, she needed a wheelchair, but we couldn't get one without a doctor's exam. Three days after the exam and x-rays, she was diagnosed with lung cancer and a tumor on her spine. We didn't open the business that spring. I took out the plants that were in the cold frames and greenhouse, potted them, priced them, and placed a note above a money box. I didn't feel it necessary to explain our closing the business. A few pots went missing, and the dirt driveway displayed signs of angry people spinning their car wheels when leaving.

It was strange to watch my business die slowly over the summer. As the gardens became weedy, a strange, cold silence settled over them. Walking out to them one evening, I could almost hear the visitors, especially one young man. He had driven in like a race car driver and stopped just short of the building. Getting out of the car, he raced around the gardens before getting back into his car and driving away. He came another time and I waited for him at the entrance of the gardens. We talked briefly before he left. Each time he came and went, his movements were slower. About the fourth or fifth time, he allowed me to give him a tour and teach him how to feel and smell the herbs. I explained a little of their lore and usage.

Weeks later, he saw me kneeling while harvesting and became

enraged. I stood and waited until he was through with his tirade. I then took him around and explained how, in harvesting, we examine a plant to check what is good about it then keep its seeds for next year's planting. We also looked at plants that didn't grow well, ascertained why they didn't and tried to learn how not to do it again. He took some seeds I had packaged for him and left.

When he came again two weeks later, his station wagon was packed full of personal possessions. He explained that on the day of his first visit, he had just received divorce papers. He hadn't known anything was wrong in his marriage. When he arrived at the gardens, he found them soothing and peaceful. He went on to say he had learned more in that one visit during harvest than in all the therapies up to that point in time. He was leaving the area with what few possessions he had left, but was leaving with a good feeling in his heart. We hugged and said "I love you" to each other. I never saw him again.

With Mom's cancer taking over our lives, we spent spring, summer, and fall taking her back and fourth between two hospitals for chemo, rehab, and blood work. I learned that the doctor had told my brother everything, including about Mom being moved to the oncology ward for chemo. My brother had left town without saying anything to us. It was then I asked the doctor to report to no one but me, her caretaker. This widened the rift between me and my siblings, but by this time, I didn't care. When Mom was on her deathbed, two sisters, black-balled years earlier by the other siblings, came and helped me nurse Mom during the final days of her life. After the pain took over, it was three days before she passed away.

Calling her *Mama* with the French pronunciation helped me to deal with her illness, to see her as someone other than my mother. I never thought about anything beyond the cancer. It was utterly invasive and absorbed our time, thoughts, finances, and social life. Indeed, we had no social life beyond her care.

My mind kept going back to a conversation we had with two customers in the store, regarding care for older parents. I had turned to Mom and said, "I don't owe you anything." Three mouths dropped before I continued, "It wasn't my idea that you birth me nor was it my idea that you raise me. Those were your choices. You're living with me because I love you, not because I'm obligated to you or because I owe you. And you know I don't give a shit what society thinks."

In a similar conversation, I had asked mom if she remembered the woman on the corner of the block, and I explained which house. I asked if she remembered going there.

"Yes, I do."

"Why did you go see her?"

"You kept disappearing, so one day I followed you."

I was stunned that Mom had done such a thing. "No way!"

"I had to make sure you were all right."

"Why didn't you say something?"

"We all need to have our secrets," was all she said.

I looked at mom a little differently after that.

And that's what counts when you provide care for someone you love. Tending my parents wasn't a burden as it would've been had I thought I owed it to them, as society would have me believe. While I tended them, I never once thought I *had* to do it. I just did it without thinking. Love needs no reason and has no season. For a couple of years after Mom's death, I shared these thoughts with others who were, more often than not, strangers. I hugged the caregivers. Patients have their needs met, but the caregivers usually don't have anyone meeting their needs. I was amazed how many men cried when I hugged them.

One sister sent a letter postmarked one hour after Mom's death, the second such letter from her in two years. This told me how she hated me; how she was glad she never had to see me again; how everyone had sat around campfires talking about suing us, etc. But this one had no impact. I simply called each sibling and read the letter aloud to them, so they'd know I knew what had gone on behind my back, and that I actually received such letters. I also said that she needed to reread the Bible, since she had quoted quite a bit out of context. A couple of them apologized, and a couple of them grew angry when she mentioned their being alcoholics.

Remembering a visit from my siblings a few years earlier, I recalled when they attacked me for being the eldest: why did I think I was so big; who did I think I was, trying to move Mom and Dad up where we were? I wrote a letter informing them I was no longer their surrogate mother, they were to turn to Mom, and I sent Mom a copy of the letter. The family divided. When we gathered a month after Mom's death for the *giveaway*, everyone was shocked by how much there was, thinking I had taken everything.

My brother had kept my father's ashes. Though two of my sisters would not stay the extra thirty minutes, the rest us drove the short distance to the bridge where our parents requested their ashes be released. We all knelt and said silent prayers as my brother threw our parents' ashes over the bridge railing into the river. The letter writer never showed at all. My brother called later to say a sister wanted my phone number. By that time, I had made up my mind about my *family*.

"When Mom died, so did my responsibilities as the eldest. Your sister is not to have my number. No one is to call me."

This was November of '89.

Phlox—Our souls are reunited

There was an incident so powerful it will go with me to my grave. I'd remember this same incident over and over again to sustain me in my marriage.

Jim and I rarely got it together enough to be of the same mind at the same time, especially about sex. One spring day at mid-morning, we walked the thirty feet to the herb farm. The four steps up to it were sixteen feet across and five feet deep, with two crab apple trees on both sides of each step, for a total of sixteen trees. On that day they were loaded with blossoms, the air so heavy with their scent it turned your stomach. We reached the top step. My parents hadn't moved in yet, and the greenhouse hadn't been built.

Jim turned toward me with that goofy look of his, wanting sex. I thought him incredible and said, "You have got to be kidding." I started chuckling, thinking about us being only two hundred feet from the main highway, hidden behind the crab apples, a red maple, and a hemlock tree.

The only available space was under the crab apple tree, which was more like a bush, on the top step. About five minutes into the lovemaking, if one can count in such an emotional state, I noticed a brilliant blue daisy-like flower next to Jim's ear. Its fragrance was a combination of vanilla extract and an exotic perfume. Two black stripes ran the length of each of the six petals. Reaching for the flower, I let go of Jim. Quickly and passionately he moved me onto the creeping phlox growing on the bank next to the steps.

At some point in our lovemaking, something ethereal enveloped us. The soft wind behaved like a feather fanning our warm bodies, an oriole sang in the maple tree, and traffic on the main highway sounded like murmuring. We had been married twenty years, and sex was sex. But, on that day, it took on an exquisiteness I have not felt before or since. It was when I looked into the sun's brightness that I had seen the blue flower. I don't know for sure how long we were down under the tree.

"Sorry, honey. Got a little excited," he said as he helped me up and cleaned off my back where I had been lying on the prickly leaves of the creeping phlox.

While both of us dressed, with our backsides to the street, I noticed red marks on his butt. "What are those marks on your ass?"

He reached toward the crab apple tree and he showed me where a bottom branch had broken. "It kept sticking my cheek. Every time I raised my butt, it stuck me, forcing me to drop down."

I giggled at the vision conjured up in my mind before saying, "Hmmm, guess I need to thank this tree for a few nice dives. And here I was admiring your new lovemaking techniques."

I told Jim about the flower and we searched among the scratchy creeping phlox. As thick as it was, I'd have been surprised if we had found the plant. While searching, I tried to remember what the leaf looked like, but couldn't remember seeing one. The flower was still vivid that night in my dreams and I still smelled it.

Two days later, while checking my reference manuals for the bloom, I remembered its scent. *How I could have smelled the one blue flower over all those crab apple blossoms?* I didn't find it. My research took me to the local library, to the college, and finally to a phone call with the dean of horticulture at the university in the middle of the state. He was no help. I gave up searching after two years and became engrossed in the herb business. Jim had forgotten the flower after the initial search.

Six years after the incident, a friend of mine, Fran, wanted to visit an artist friend. Making it a ladies day, we had a special lunch before driving over to his studio. Ben, at eighty-two, could have been Albert Einstein's twin, with his wild white hair sticking out all over his head, and blue-veined, transparent skin stretching over a thin, frail skeleton. What struck me most was the lack of wrinkles on his baby face.

I left them alone to play catch-up. I was wandering around his studio, marveling at his art, when I spied a covered easel standing in the corner. Seeing they were still occupied, I decided to risk a glance under the cover. I lifted the fabric and…blackness.

"Are you all right, Lady?" Fran, looking worried, had knelt down and handed me a glass of water.

"What happened? Did I faint?" After taking a mental inventory of my body, I stood and walked toward the offered chair. *The last thing I remembered…* I glanced toward the easel. With the cover thrown back, I saw an exact replica of my blue flower; except this one covered an 11" x18" canvas.

"Where did you see that flower child?" Ben leaned toward me with a look of humor on his face.

I was irritated and handed him the empty glass. "I didn't see it anywhere. It doesn't exist." I didn't like my privacy being invaded. I'd never told anyone about the morning under the crab apple trees. It was something special and I wanted to keep it to myself.

Ignoring me, he continued, his eyes twinkling. "You're not the only one who has seen that flower. It has been seen by me and my wife and two other couples that I know of. One is in England, and the other is in Japan. This flower is special, you know."

It was Fran's turn to sit down on the floor.

Staring at the canvas, I said, "I searched for two years for that flower. I couldn't find it anywhere. I even called the Horticulture Department at the Michigan State University." I turned toward him and saw he was smiling ear to ear. "What's so special about this flower?"

Leaning closer, he almost whispered, "What did it smell like?"

"Vanilla extract…"

"…and exotic perfume?" he whispered.

"Yes. I swear I can still smell it." I whispered, "Please, what does it mean?"

He pulled up a chair and sat down. "For lack of a better title, the *New Age* community says it is a gift from the *other side*."

“The other side of what?”

“Some will tell you there is a thin veil between this reality and the one on the other side, the one you enter into when you pass over. There are certain times in our reality, during acts of total or pure love when the strength of the giving opens a portal. I think it quite interesting that all of us saw the exact same flower. And you’re right, it doesn’t exist. At least, not in this reality.”

“Our whole lovemaking took on something surreal that day. It was beautiful, actually.” Remembering the sensations, I fell to daydreaming until Ben startled me out of it.

“I know exactly how you feel. Would you like a print of the painting?”

The offer threw me and I sat quietly for a moment. “No, thank you. I would be compelled to frame it only to have to explain it to others. I think I’d rather save the experience in my mind and heart. It still feels special.”

We thanked Ben. Soon after our meeting, he died. I never forgot his painting and wished I had taken him up on his offer. I can share with you that to this day I know for a fact that this gift from the other side was the only reason I stayed with my husband when we started having major problems years later.

That was the summer we had the canoe accident that opened doors to a spirituality I never knew existed within me. And this spirituality showed me why we received the gift of the flower and several other gifts I alone received.

✳

Goldenrod—Be cautious

After six months of remodeling the inside of the house, Mom's phantom wheelchair still whispered through the house. One night, about nine months after her death, I heard her call my name. Waking out of a dead sleep, I went to our bedroom door to see what she wanted. Her voice had been so real I was surprised to find she wasn't sitting in her wheelchair on the other side of the door. I shook my head over the idea that we still closed our bedroom door. We were the only ones living in the house.

We didn't reopen the greenhouse or the store. I had no desire to continue them. And it would take three employees to do the work Mom and I had done—we had worked that well together. I finished my mini-degree in data processing, but my heart wasn't into going back to the university. While in business, we had built a freestanding building for the herb shop and had shut down the natural foods part. The old store was converted into a large studio/classroom. But now it stood empty except for a few items stored in it. The storeroom that had been the classroom in the beginning of the business now stood nearly empty, too. In the old store, converted into a studio, I wove baskets now and then for galleries, thinking I would get back into the art world. But I had lost the heart for that as well.

The silence in the house became deafening and the gardens were no longer enjoyable. When I started roaming our property, looking for something to do, I decided it was time to go back to work. I worked in two office manager positions in two years before landing the third job in a corporation. Thinking I was hired as a clerk, within a week I realized I was being trained as the president's left hand. But his right hand didn't appreciate my acting as counselor to the divorcing president, so she fired me.

The position I had been training for reminded me of something a seer had said to me years earlier. Virtually a stranger to me, he didn't hesitate to tell me I would either be a liaison between a president and the outside world, or walk a spiritual path. That thought crept to the front of my mind as I drove home that day. I was still in shock at having been fired for the first time in my life. Jim was surprised to see me home early, and I told him what had happened. I expected him to be angry because it would mean less money—my pay had been good. He said he was sorry and discussed my signing up for unemployment compensation. I went but didn't think there was a snowball's chance of getting anything; but it did support me for a year.

Six months later I met the president's right hand in the farmer's market. She informed me that she and the president had married and honeymooned in Africa. The sympathy I felt toward her surprised me as I watched her walk away, sash-shaying her hips.

I spent the next two years in retrospection. Closing the business I had created from the ground up was synonymous with losing another child. I had created it from the beginning and nurtured it, only to watch it weaken and die. My parents' deaths hit me especially hard. I had spent years trying to find a place where we could all live together and help them gain some semblance of peace, only to watch them succumb. I thought about the degree I had obtained to get a good position in the work force, only to lose the job through jealousy and greed of another.

I also thought of my son and what little contact we had with him. After our grandson was abused by his stepmother, the two of them had spent a month with us. Our grandson stayed another two months. We didn't have much contact with either of them after that. Jim and I decided to take the retirement package the state had offered, since his position was disappearing through privatization. There was nothing to keep us in Michigan.

The following spring, I went to Kentucky where I was born. I visited my niece before going on to visit an acquaintance in the mountains in Tennessee. Jim visited his favorite brother in his hometown in Michigan. After two days in the mountains I was contacted by a sheriff's deputy because my friend had no phone. Jim had had a heart attack and was in the hospital. Two days later I took Jim to a cardiac hospital near where we lived. His quadruple by-pass surgery took place the following Tuesday.

We addressed the 'dying' issue the night before the surgery.

"You need to get through this because I want you to see Tennessee. It would be a nice place to live."

"Honey, if I get through this we'll go wherever you want."

He'll tell you I took advantage of him and I'm not sure I didn't. His heart attack was on his April birthday and by August we were in Tennessee. Within a year, we found the property we wanted and had it registered before we left on Good Friday of '93. I went back home and packed what I could, eager to get on with a new life.

Nearly eighteen months passed and our Michigan property still hadn't sold.

One day, looking around the studio, I saw all the dried materials for potpourri, hats, and wreaths; the reeds and natural fibers for basket weaving; the loom and yarns, and the spinning wheel in the corner. Looking at each section of the studio, I remembered all the workshops I'd given. I remembered in particular the first day I picked up someone's bag of potpourri and received an image. I related what it was and to everyone's amazement, my own included, I was correct. After that I played at *reading* what others created.

Standing in that studio, I realized I had a gift and knew I had to explore my inner self for other gifts. I spent the next two weeks selling everything in my studio. It had been my place of creation, and I couldn't understand why I felt compelled so strongly to sell my baby. But I did as I was guided. Two months later, the house sold and two weeks after that, we were driving down to Tennessee hauling a fully loaded twelve-foot U-Haul trailer.

This was not to be a pivotal change in my life, but a change so drastic as to nearly cost me my life.

Purple Hyacinth—Please forgive me

We built in the Clinch Mountains near the Kentucky border and I felt I was moving back home, close to where I was born. I even started attending my family reunion and learned I had a *sack full* of relatives. I had searched my whole life for a place to call home. I'd never felt comfortable in Michigan. I felt it was a place where I had bided my time. My heart was full of expectations and immediately warmed anew at the sight of the mountains.

We moved into a mobile home while we built our monolithic dome. Not comfortable after a neighbor saw someone on the property before dawn, we moved into a small building we had built for storage. We bought another building for storage and set it up on the property, then made another trip to Michigan to clean out one of two large storage units.

Once the dome was built, we took our time to move in and finish the inside. I did the electrical work, and an electrician checked the more complicated wiring. All in all, we did a very good job for two people who didn't know what they were doing and were doing it by the seat of their pants. It didn't take us long to realize Jim's retirement income wasn't going to go far. We had to get a mortgage and I had to go back to work.

Almost from the time we moved into the mountains, I became really irritable. The *it* I had kept ahead of for years had caught up to me again. *It* was stronger this time, and my bitchiness worsened. I picked on Jim for everything without provocation. Looking back on it, I wonder why he even stayed with me. He wasn't all that crazy about moving out of Michigan and voiced that objection more than once.

I cannot remember a time when I wasn't angry about something. Bar hopping became the norm on Fridays and Saturdays. I drank a six-pack a day and was game for anything, even an affair with a man in a neighboring county. It was exciting, the sneaking around and the meetings. I didn't know what was going on with me. I felt that time between my military discharge and Tennessee had been a pleasant dream from another life, that what I was experiencing now was just a continuation of my Navy way of life. I rarely felt guilty about my neglecting Jim, and when I did, I dismissed it immediately.

I lived in four worlds: one filled with locals speaking Southern; one filled with *outsiders* and their non-Southern accents, a lot of whom were college educated; the third was filled with male drinkers and users; and the fourth world was my life in the dome, from which

I tried to escape as much as possible because it was so boring. I also started smoking again, having quit over twenty years ago.

There were times of respite. I developed a relationship with a country woman who had a kind demeanor and a soft humor, and who became my surrogate mother. I met her while trying to buy country butter and buttermilk, and she was the last in the county to churn her own butter. In many ways, she's part of a dying breed of people, who, though they may not agree with what you say or do, will do what they can for you because their faith is stronger than others' religious hypocrisy.

Then there was my mechanic. He's younger than my son but most times, had a wisdom that sometimes surprised me. Many nights I went to his garage for a laugh or two while he worked. I also went four-wheeling with him and his family and other friends. Evenings in that garage, talking and laughing, was more than an escape from my reality, sometimes it was my life saver. He also took away some of the fears that tried to creep in after I had small accidents or when I was stranded and had to be towed in.

Also, there was an elderly gentleman whom I called Pappy. But then, he was Pappy to everyone. He and his wife, along with their five children, were kind to me and were generous with their love. Pappy was the father and grandfather I never had. I'm sure some of his children didn't understand our relationship, but that was all right. I do know some of the neighbors didn't think much of it, but that didn't matter either. I felt bad for Pappy when his wife died. He's still a lost soul without her.

For four years, my life remained chaotic until one night I lay in bed, crying. I hadn't been able to cry for a very long time. The tears were painful, and I was angry, lonely, and hurting but didn't know why. Jim had been totally beside himself for quite awhile; I never had a good thing to say to him anymore. This night, I was so desperate that for the first time since hearing the Citadel bell I entertained the idea of escaping out of this world.

"God, please take my dark thoughts, my alcohol, my cigarettes, and my anger—or take me. I can't go on anymore," I prayed.

Within two months I planned a bonfire party with selected friends. The party wasn't my idea, but that of Guidance, my guardian angel. By this time Guidance and I conversed regularly and I came to rely on him for counseling and to be there to hear my tirades—not that *I* ever listened. I bought fireworks and, with the help of a friend, cleaned up the house like I had never cleaned it before. I even built shelves alongside the bathtub, a project I had put off for three years.

The night of the party, I stood outside the circle and was amazed at the diversity of the people I knew. I was equally amazed at how little I knew them. On some level, I wanted very much to get closer to them, but couldn't. I haven't allowed myself to get close to anyone after a close friend of ten years dumped me when I was no longer of use to her.

Everyone commented on how much they were enjoying themselves. They sat five feet from the fire when it was first lit, inching their way closer as the night progressed and the fire burned smaller. Halfway through the night, this encouraged intimacy as we told small stories, laughed, sang, and drummed. I had given a few parties, and though this one was the first in Tennessee, I thought it was the best of all.

I should have realized by now that when things go right, they're going to go bad. The party was Saturday, and I was scheduled to go on a three-day retreat, Tuesday through Thursday. Finished with it on Wednesday, I left in the misty rain and drove home. After arriving, I decided to go get the truck-bed cover from a friend. I hadn't paid for it, but I was in the mood to pick it up, and I knew my friend would allow me to pay at the end of the week.

I drove the Ranger we had bought at an auction two months earlier. It was in excellent condition but badly needed new tires. We couldn't afford them and felt we could wait. As I put on my left blinker to turn down the road, I became irritated at having to wait for an oncoming car. I turned the corner and had traveled about a mile when I turned my steering wheel left into the slight curve. My wheels didn't turn.

At first, my mind registered, "Oh, shit. I'm not going to hold the road." Then time shifted into slow motion.

Crossing in front of a house, I traveled two hundred feet that felt more like a mile. Every time I bounced and came back down onto the seat, my foot hit the gas pedal. So I let go of the steering wheel. I slid over into the passenger seat then onto the floor, facing the driver's side. The truck bounced hard, and I came up off the floor and hit the windshield with the right side of my head, breaking my eye glasses. Down I went again only to bounce back up again and impacted the windshield a second time when the truck hit a five-foot ditch.

Through blurred vision, I saw a police car moving away. Sheer panic forced my arm upward to push on the truck's horn and I kept up the pressure until I lost strength. Sitting on the floor in the lonely silence, I remembered my prayer asking God to take me. I hadn't specified how, so I felt maybe I deserved this. My body began to hurt, especially my abdomen, as a heavy fatigue settled over me. I felt more tired than I had ever felt in my life. One eye already closed, I closed the other one and waited.

"Lady! Lady, are you all right?"

The voice registered in my foggy brain. I opened my eyes and saw a deputy's uniform. Grabbing hold of the steering wheel, I sat up again in the driver's seat after two attempts.

The deputy struggled to stand upright in the ditch as he leaned over and opened the door. "Lady, don't do that. Stay still. The ambulance is on its way. I won't leave you until they get here"

Thank you, God. I now realize I didn't mean it. I tried to put my head on my arm on the steering wheel but the windshield was in the way. The front end of the truck had bent upward when it hit the side of the ditch. Had I been going any faster, the truck would have folded into a V with me caught in the middle. I also noticed the windshield had been shattered from the inside.

Someone handed the deputy a towel, "Here use this towel." Then in a louder voice, the unknown man said, "Lady, don't rub your eye. Just use the towel to blot the blood."

Blood?!! A blurred image jumped into my mind, but what little consciousness I had pushed it back down. Fading in and out of conscious, I hurt but couldn't quite figure out where. Pain just registered somewhere in my body. I felt my head swell and reached up to scratch my eye.

"Don't do that." The deputy pulled my hand away and in a gentler voice said. "Please, don't do that. Just hold on. I hear the ambulance now."

The truck jerked and I panicked anew, my hand flying out for support.

"I have her hitched up now. The truck won't topple over." A new voice said.

Topple over?!! I couldn't think. I wanted to ask questions, but I felt I'd have to walk a hundred miles back to reach these people. *So what was I going to ask?*

"It's okay Lady. Your truck is stabilized now and won't roll forward. The ambulance is here. Please, don't move. Let us do the work."

I fell in love with that deputy as I tossed out a mental prayer of gratitude that I'd lost weight again. It was a hard task, but the four men placed me on a backboard. And my mind registered the brace around my neck as someone strapped my head to the board.

I blacked out.

Someone whispered, "Her blood pressure is seventy over fifty-five. You know I think we have something here."

I came to enough to hear someone say, "I'm cutting off her clothes now."

Another voice said, "Okay, I'll take out the rest of the glass out of her face."

Glass in my face?

A loud voice said, "Lady, are you there?"

From the waist up he looked like he wore a space suite with his helmet closed. It took me a long time to answer, and all that came out was a grunt before I passed out again.

Loud! The chopper ride was loud. The sound of the rotor blades echoed in my head as I floated on air as well as in and out of consciousness; sometimes in this world, sometimes in the other world.

"I need another port site."

My eyes flew open and I saw a young man standing alongside my gurney. "Bucko, I have been stuck fourteen times." *Had I actually counted?* "You had better get it right the first time or I'm going to take you down." I passed out again.

I opened my eyes when I felt pain in my groin area. The same young man finished shoving a catheter needle all the way in. He said nothing as he stared at me, but I felt his finger flick my leg and sensed him saying, "How's that, bitch?" I passed out again.

When I regained consciousness, I knew I was in ICU. I was there for four days before being transferred to the tenth floor for head trauma. That night the stitches were removed from my right eye lid. My eye glasses had broken in two and part of the lenses went into my right eye lid, though the membrane under it was not torn. I had asked why my eye hadn't been sewn up in surgery and was told, "No sense in sewing up a corpse." My friends told me I was listed as Seriously Critical—death being the next stage down.

By Sunday night, I had taken on an irritating cough. Afraid by Monday that the stitches might be coming loose, I had asked the nurse to check to make sure my incision was still in tact. The surgeon had cut me from sternum to bikini line searching for internal bleeding. He took out an inch and a half of my small intestines that had burst in the accident.

Shaking her head in disbelief, she said, "My God, Lady, your stitches have healed."

My body healed faster than I had ever seen it heal before. I had been walking since Sunday to keep down the gas. When I was told the pain medicine created gas, I didn't take it any more. However, my mind was another issue. I had no memory of anyone other than those who visited me in ICU and while I was on the floor.

For a month afterwards, I oriented myself with my surroundings, which were familiar, yet not familiar. It was the same with the visitors and my husband. I felt I had gone for a drive in the Ranger, now totaled, and woke up in a parallel, surreal universe.

Later, riding around the town, people looked familiar to me, but I had no idea what kind of relationship I had with them. By the end of the month, things were better, but I still had memory problems and became wary of people because of them.

*

Buck Bean—Calm repose

It took two and half years for me to gain back what memory I thought I'd lost. From mid-July into August of 2002, I began remembering at a faster rate. I didn't have headaches but experienced nausea when a lot of memories hit me at once. As I didn't know the size of my memory bank before the accident, I couldn't determine how much of it I had regained or how much of it was still lost. My saving graces were playing games on the computer as fast as I could and doing crossword puzzles. Today, they're still a bit of an obsession.

Did I get what I prayed for? The day of the accident was the last day I smoked. I tried cigarettes occasionally, but they tasted nasty after the first drag. I still drank, but my consumption went way down, for a while.

Feeling confident in my mental abilities, I decided to open a non-profit, 501c educational center that would include a program for dyslexia and summer day camps. It took nearly a year to get everything in place, and I was really quite proud at having done all the work from incorporation documents and a board of directors to the state-accepted campground, designed for educational programs, with contacts across the country. My county of residence didn't want anything to do with my program. And I couldn't get a press release. I have my suspicions about that, but I now look upon the whole thing as universal guidance.

In April, 2003, I took a certification course to be a Redirecting Children's Behavior Instructor. It's a program designed to teach parents the four emotions they feel when their children act out; emotions that will determine how to redirect their children's behaviors. This parenting program was created by Kathy Kvols, founder and director of INCAF (International Network for Children and Families). They now have on-line parenting tips. This foundation also has a Redirecting a Cooperative Classroom, in which I was also certified, and Redirecting Corporate America. In six months of research, this was the best parenting program I had found that actually demonstrated, in four to six weeks, problem-solving solutions parents could use for the rest of their children's lives, while at the same time teaching children how to make responsible choices.

INCAF highly recommends that an instructor go through a self-help program before standing before their first class. While role-playing in the training program, I was the parent confronted by an angry child. I was dumbstruck and backed away from the adult playing the child. This had never happened before. That night I dreamed of the day Mom allowed me to repay the one dollar that caused such a violent argument between us.

Because of the dream, I attended a UYO (Understanding Yourself and Others) workshop for a very intense weekend offered by Global Relationship Center in Atlanta, GA. We are assigned an Angel and surrounded by people acting as Angels who brought us water, took us to lunch, literally met our every need throughout the weekend. Two months later, I went back to the UYO as an Angel. Both workshops gave me enough insight to let go of my son when he was in a crisis and allow him to make his own choices. Within three months, he also attended both weekends.

In the meantime, I continued working on my educational center with the intention of opening that fall, with the day camps to follow the next summer. My drinking picked up again. My nerves were raw and I found myself driving around to keep from harping on Jim. The dark thoughts were gone and the intense anger had left as well. But the intense desire to run—from what, I didn't know—stayed with me. I no longer looked at it as the *it*. But I couldn't name what it was, either.

Friday, August 8, 2003, I went into the studio to finish the drainpipe to the sink. At 8 a.m. I got my tools together and the bag of fittings for the drain and pipe, along with the PVC cleaner and glue. My brain slowly turned to mush as I stood and looked around, wondering what I needed to do first. My mental abilities left me as if someone had waved a magic wand above my head and wished them gone.

Thinking everything was ready, I cut the water line and was aghast to see it gush like a dam had burst. My brain wouldn't register where the turnoff valve was located. I just knew it wasn't in the studio. I ran into the dome to turn off the pump, and on the way back, passing the guest room attached to the studio, I remembered the turn-off valve was in there, under the sink.

The studio had standing water across half of the floor. I mopped up a five-gallon bucket of water. Walking to the door, I spilled it. I couldn't see anything on the floor I could have tripped over. I mopped up another bucketful and spilled it again. I did this two more times. The amazing thing was, I didn't cuss, didn't get angry; didn't even get upset. I had unknowingly gone into my robotic mode. I never even questioned why I hadn't turned the water off first.

The day wore on as I mopped up the floor. It takes a while to pick up gallons and gallons of water with a small mop. I finally opened the drainpipe package and read the directions. My brain couldn't take them in. The longer I stood there the more my brain's numbness seeped down through my body. *I plumbed the dome sinks and the guest room. Surely, I can do this.* But I couldn't.

A few hours later, after dropping the purple PVC cleaner on the floor, then the glue, I sat on the floor and stared at the mess. Looking around me, I tried to figure out what was happening. When I put together two pipe sections wrong, I set them down and went into the dome and had two Rum and Cokes. I discovered I had been out in the dome for nine hours trying to do a forty-minute plumbing job.

After the rum and Cokes I went back to the studio, determined not to come out until the pipe was in place. An hour later, I shoved the sink back into place and pushed the drain pipe in. It didn't fit. A few more aggressive shoves and it went into place. There was still no swearing and no anger. I felt no emotions, whatsoever. Something had shut me down.

I had showered by the time Jim came in. "Are you all right?" he asked, staring at me.

"I don't know. I'll be outside for a while."

He silently watched me as I closed the door. I sat outside for the longest time trying to figure out what was going on and where my senses had gone. I had another Rum and Coke. It was strange not to crave a cigarette.

Saturday, my grandson Kris arrived with his girlfriend. They didn't stay long because they wanted to go sightseeing. My mood not conducive to congenial company, I stayed by myself and roamed the house. I rechecked the drainpipe and found it satisfactory. I also found a coupling to fix where I had cut the water line. This time I didn't spill anything, but I still couldn't feel anything, either.

That night I didn't sleep, I just tossed and turned. The next morning, Sunday, I fixed breakfast while Kris and his girlfriend packed to go back home. Phil arrived in time for breakfast. There was soft talk around the table, but I was I was still in my own world. By noon everyone had gone; Kris and his girl had left for home and Phil, and Jim had gone golfing. I went out to the studio to clean up the remaining mess from Friday. I had no idea it would be the last time for quite a long time. The flashback I had that afternoon would put me in the VA hospital.

⁕

Rosemary—Remembrance

My eyes still closed, I saw BG pick me up, and wrap the sheet around me and carry me to the door. He was such a gentle giant, and I had totally forgotten him. I wondered if he was the one who beat my rapist. Scenes from the Navy were moving across my inner vision. BG was Frank's best friend, and they were the first sailors I met when I transferred to the second base. I had been raped in that motel room and BG carried me away with Frank following him. *I wonder how they knew where I was?*

The bed I was in felt comfortable but I knew it wasn't mine. I opened my eyes all the way and scanned the room. I was wearing a hospital gown and looked for the closet to find my clothes. Not seeing anything but walls, I rested my head against the pillow.

I don't remember falling asleep.

Hearing someone, I glanced at the door and watched five people walk into the room, three men and two women. They pulled up chairs. *Where did those come from?* They sat in a semicircle. When they were settled, they just stared at me, some with their chins resting in their palms. No one said a word.

What the hell is this about?

I rose up on my right elbow and broke the silence with, "I don't know what you folks have in mind, but I need to be out of here before the weekend, to go to Atlanta."

I wish to hell they would say something. What am I supposed to do, or say?

I tried again, "I need to support my son, you see. He's doing a UYO class."

Still no one moved. *Why don't they talk?*

I sat up, placed my feet on the floor, and stared at my toes. "Well, I guess I could let it go and think of myself." Intuiting what I had just said aloud, my mind went blank.

"Now we can talk. I'm Dr. David Hensley and this is your psychiatric team." He pointed as he went around the arc and introduced everyone in turn. "How are you feeling?"

"Better than when I came in. What was in that pill, anyway? I don't remember anything."

"We call it our miracle wonder," said Mike, the physician's assistant.

"So what happens now?"

"We're going to move you into the main hospital this morning. In the meantime, Alice here will take down some information for us and get you ready to move." He turned to leave but stopped and looked back at me. "You know, you're going to be all right."

I stared at him. *I'm in a psychiatric ward where I was given a pill that took a day out of my miserable life; a "team" of people marched into my room in lockdown, on cue, as though watching me on camera and waiting for me to wake up; and that's supposed to make me feel better?*

I rose from my bed. "Where are my clothes?"

Ruth, the social worker, answered, "Lady, you'll be wearing pajamas like these for a few days." She handed me a pair of sturdy cotton burgundy pajamas. They snapped up the front of the long-sleeved top, with a snap fly in the pants.

I guess they don't expect many women in here. I looked up in time to see her back as she left the room. *Did she say a few days…?*

They moved me out of lockdown into a private, spacious room with a large bathroom. In one corner, head high, was a single corner shelf holding one book, *Gordon's Passage*. Curious, I picked it up and read the back cover. "Someone wrongfully sent to prison before being shipped off to Australia." *How appropriate!* I tucked the book under my arm like a security blanket and walked out into the hall to explore.

Seeing that one of the two people at the nurses' station was a female, I asked her, "Is there someplace quiet where I can read, please?"

"There's the lounge area down the hall, or the cafeteria. But I think Dr. Hensley wants to see you," and she got up and disappeared through a closed door behind her.

I stood and waited. The remaining male nurse smiled and I averted my eyes. *What's the matter with you, woman? He's just a man.*

Not being able to look at a man was new for me. I used to avidly seek their company.

Dr. Hensley came out, smiling, and pointed toward a door right across from the nurses' station. "How are you feeling? Are you in a private room?" he asked in a bright voice.

"Yes." I wrapped the book in my arms like it was a stuffed teddy bear.

"Today we'd like to get some blood samples. Have you been tested for hepatitis?"

"I don't know. Am I going to always wear pajamas? I couldn't find my clothes."

"The nurse has put them away. Once we get to know you better, you can have them back."

"What do you mean get to know me better?" Small anxieties fluttered in my stomach.

"We need to talk with you about your flashback, Lady. Learn what happened and determine how we can help you." He must have seen something in my face. "It's okay. We understand these things can be a shock.

Really! And when was the last time you had your vagina blown out? "How long is this going to take? I mean…how long am I going to be in here?"

"Sometimes a week, sometimes longer. We get some history. We make sure you are doing all right before you have visitors."

"My husband can't see me?" My voice rose as the small anxieties grew bigger.

"Not today or tomorrow, maybe Wednesday. We want to make sure you aren't suicidal or homicidal. Can you understand that?"

"Yes. But you need to understand something." My voice grew hard as I tapped my finger on his desk. I looked him in the eye and said, "I am not suicidal. When I was in the ER, I was asked if I wanted to kill someone. I responded yes and named them. But even they aren't worth my going to jail."

"Those are the things we need to talk about. Do you hold them responsible for you being here?" His eyes looked straight into mine, as though he could see right into my brain, searching.

"No. I'm here for something else. I lost control in the ER. Actually, I don't know what happened. That wasn't me." *Hell no, that wasn't me. But if not me, then who?*

"You had a full-blown anxiety attack, Lady. I believe you mentioned something about a lot of blood…?"

And again, with the piercing gaze. But I couldn't look into his eyes this time. *What am I feeling here?*

Lowering my head I touched the bottom snap of my pajamas with one finger and began playing with it. "Yes. A lot of blood, all over the place, on me, the bed, the floor…" My voice trailed off as I saw the blood in my mind's eye. My hands shook. "That was me on the bed, naked." I wiped tears off my face. "I think what scared me more than anything was that my vagina hurt. It was so painful, I fell to my knees. It-it was like I was there, in the scene. I was watching, yet I was on the bed." Touching the corner of the desk, I whispered, "How can someone watch a movie and be in it at the same time? It makes no sense."

"It's called a flashback. Some—."

"I don't care what it's called. I don't know that person." My voice rose. "How could something like that have happened to me and I don't remember it?" *That wasn't me. That's for damn sure. No one could have hurt me like that and got away with it. No one! Please, God, help me. Make me wake up from this nightmare.*

"Some people can be so traumatized that their mind blocks it out. But the subconscious doesn't forget. Sometimes the memory sneaks up on you, like yours did you." His voice was gentle, his demeanor kind. "Can you tell me what you remember?"

I related the same thing I'd told the psychiatrist in the ER the day before. While he sat there and took notes, images played in the fog in my head, but nothing focused.

"Is there anything else?" he asked, watching me and still smiling gently.

I snapped, "Isn't that enough?" I didn't care that I was being sarcastic. *Am I going to have to deal with these people staring at me the whole time I'm here? And what's with the smiling? Is that a requirement?*

He sat there waiting, ignoring my tone. "We can talk more about it tomorrow. Today, they'll do some blood work. Your caseworker will also be paying you a visit." *That smile is getting a little old.* "Are there any questions?"

"Is there a quiet room other than my room, the lounge or the cafeteria?" At some point since I woke up that morning, I had acquiesced to the idea of staying in the hospital for a few days.

"Sure, I'll show it to you." He got up and opened the door, motioning for me to go first. "It's right around this corner." We turned left out of his office and around the corner, toward lockdown. I halted immediately. *I'm not going to lockdown. I don't care how quiet it is.* But the doctor, behind me, had stopped and stood at a door on the left that I hadn't seen. The room must have been directly on the other side of his office.

I gasped and smiled when he opened it. "How lovely! "

The four walls of the small room were covered with a mural of a faraway place, with vines in the foreground. Situated just to the right of the door was an end table with a tall lamp. Next to it was a burgundy, fan-back chair with a matching foot stool.

Perfect! "Thank you so much. If anyone is looking for me, this is where I'll be." He seemed pleased with himself for making me happy. With the door closed, I sat down in the chair and found it comfortable. *Music would be a nice escape.* I rose from the chair, went to the radio in the bookcase in the corner, and turned on classical music. Relaxing in the chair, I felt the book in my hand and opened it. A few minutes later I laid it in my lap when I got to the end of the page, not remembering anything I had just read.

I leaned back and allowed the tension to leave my shoulders. *It's so strange to feel comfortable in a psychiatric ward in a hosp....* I blinked my eyes, not believing my mental image. I was reading a piece of paper in my head. It was one of my discharge documents with two dates, one month apart, and it indicated I had been in a psychiatric ward. Images of a calendar now came into view. Not certain where the assured knowledge came from, I now knew the rape had taken place very soon after I had transferred to the new base. I was hospitalized in July and August.

My mind scanned the calendar in my head, moving across the days. I went AWOL at the end of August and had my Captain's Mast in September. I was discharged in October. No matter how hard I tried to remember what happened in April, May, and June, nothing appeared. Yet I knew, within my gut, the scenes in my flashback weren't all that had happened to me.

My internal camera continued clicking off stop-frame images: scenes with my roommate; hitchhiking while AWOL; the trip back on the plane. Everything was falling into place, like slides dropping into slots in sequential order. *At least now I know why I was in the hospital.* I felt relief at the thought, but there was no comfort.

I opened my eyes and looked at the clock on the wall. Only fifteen minutes had passed. *God, it feels like a lifetime.* I felt tears on my cheeks. My hands were hurting and I looked down. The knuckles on both hands were white from grasping the arms of the chair. Was it fear or anger? I didn't know. *How can someone suppress such memories? I wouldn't have allowed such a thing to happen to me. Perhaps I'm remembering someone else's horror?* But I knew it was my life, my horror. I remembered the yellow cast in the room where my bloody body lay on the bed. Intuitively, from that inner place where there is certainty without question, I knew that to be the reason I never cared for the color yellow.

When the door opened, the book flew out of my lap as I yelled out from a semi-dreaming state, "Leave me alone! "

The woman, too, jumped. "Oh, I'm so sorry. I didn't mean to startle you." Her face showed concern. "I'm Mrs. Ames, your caseworker. Are you all right?"

Of course you are. I shoved the footstool away from my chair and stretched out my trembling hand, offering her the stool, as I willed my insides to a state of calm.

"I see you found a nice room. I didn't know this was here."

I don't know what she wants, but at least she's not staring at me. I put one elbow on the arm of the chair, rested my chin on my fist, and waited.

She came to the point. "I'm here to answer any questions you may have regarding your stay in the hospital. If you have any problems with any one or anything, I'm here to help you with that. Is there anything you wish to discuss?"

"What privileges do I have? I know I'm confined to this ward and—"

"No, you're not."

"Excuse me?" I perked up.

"You can go off this ward with permission of the staff. You'll be wearing what you're now wearing until you get your street clothes. But you can go get a newspaper or go to the cafeteria. You just can't leave the hospital."

I brightened at the idea of leaving the ward, until something obscure tried to crawl forward into my mind and I pushed it back. I didn't want to deal with it.

"It isn't our intention to make you a prisoner here. We just want to figure out what's going on and come up with a program to help you through it. Let me know if there's anything you wish to discuss." She gave me her card and quietly closed the door behind her.

I sensed she was genuine, but I still couldn't bring myself to trust her. That surprised me. Until recently, I had trusted everyone.

Retrieving my book, I waited for the door to open again. When it didn't I sat back in the chair until an awareness seeped into my mind. I realized I had always jumped at sudden movements or noises. Then fear crept into my brain. What other secrets was my mind keeping from me? Exhaling on a deep sigh, I melted into the chair and let the book rest on my lap while I closed my eyes. *When did I last rest? Really rest?* I began to wonder if that little pill I had taken the day before also took away my zombie state.

All of Friday had been bizarre. Everyone had left early, leaving me time to hook up the drainpipe and the hot and cold lines to the faucet to the studio sink. I'd done that project several times over the years, so it should have been a snap.

After everyone left, the whole place had taken on an eerie silence, like a void. I couldn't remember hearing traffic in front of the dome. My brain had operated sluggishly; my thoughts waded through a quagmire. It didn't occur to me now to feel stupid about not remembering because my brain simply hadn't registered anything. I couldn't remember thinking anything all the while I was on my knees sopping up water. My brain had gone on vacation and left my body behind.

My book flew to the other side of the foot stool at the sound of the door opening again. *My heart can't stand much more of this.* It was still pounding when yet another woman stuck her head around the edge and asked, "Hi, are you Lady?" When I mutely nodded my head, she continued, "May we go to your room and take some blood please?"

I picked up the book and silently followed her. *Did I sleep the morning away? My God, I'm tense.* The clock on the wall indicated it was only eleven, not even lunchtime yet.

When I walked into the cafeteria, it was obvious that every diner had their own table. One man was totally absorbed in something invisible on the surface of his. He never looked up from that one spot, not even when his tray was placed in front of him. Another man rolled his head around in circles. He intrigued me until I realized he wasn't going to hum a mantra. Another younger man, whom I remembered seeing behind the lounge door windows when I was admitted, stole furtive glances. Yet another man sat at his table behind the square column in the middle of the room, trying his best to disappear but his size forbade it. Lunch was surprisingly tasty.

I spent the rest of the day exploring the hall and reading the bulletin boards. I didn't want to venture into the lounge area; I knew the men were in there. Well spaced men at lunch was one thing, but I wasn't ready for them en masse just yet. By the time I went to bed that night, my vital signs were normal. I felt tired and declined a sleeping pill.

Pine—Hope, pity

By the end of the next day I had a routine and was comfortable walking around in my small world with a book in my hand, reading the bulletin boards—again. Something else had happened since the weekend. My memory wasn't right. I knew I had read the bulletins, but I couldn't remember them. Even making an effort with word association, my brain would not retain them. It was as though someone had shut the vault door on my short-term memory bank.

I went to my lovely quiet room often and sat in the fan-back chair to read or listen to the radio. I had talks with my psychiatric PA; another talk with the patient advocate; gave more information to this one, to that one. I went downstairs in my burgundy pajamas and dared anyone to say anything to me. But my little trek went without incident and I found myself in the elevator smiling like a simpleton. It only confused me when I tried to comprehend why a tiny ignored act of defiance should amuse me. *Perhaps I've stepped through more than one door in this wonderland and don't know it.*

On the third day, Wednesday, Jim came. The clothes and purse he brought for me had to be given to the nurse, and I would get them after they were checked. *Right! This is the psych ward.* Jim and I visited a few minutes before going downstairs to the cafeteria. It was strange, really, the two of us sitting in a cafeteria, me in men's pajamas with Jim sitting across from me, and the two of us talking as though we were in a restaurant and nothing had happened. I took the initiative and asked how he had been doing.

"Barb and I talked for a long time. She's tried to explain to me, but I still don't know if I understand all that's happening." His fatigued voice indicated he hadn't been sleeping.

That reminded me of how *well* I had been sleeping, better than in years. Poor Jim! He was trying so hard to understand something for which neither of us had a clue.

Touching his hand, I said "Honey, I was violently raped forty years ago. I suppressed it until now." I knew my voice was tense. "I don't know why it came out now. Truth be known, if I hadn't heard myself say it, I'd swear it happened to someone else. What scares me is that this flashback might not be the only one."

I didn't want to tell him that. But on an intuitive level I knew there was something else hiding back there in the dark recesses of my mind, trying it's best to come forward.

"They say if I go through therapy, I'll be on the medication for about a year. If I don't go through therapy, I'll be on the medication for the rest of my life. That medication is wicked stuff. I'm sick most of the time."

"Have they told you when you can leave?" He was scared.

"They're talking about Friday." *I don't really want to leave my sanctuary.* I hurriedly went on to ask about any phone calls the mail, visitors. *Visitors! Now there's a laugh.* "Do you want to go for a walk?"

He responded by getting up and reaching for my hand. I sensed the little boy in him and his wanting things back to normal, not that we'd had a normal life since we moved to the Tennessee mountains. In fact, we had moved into an area where the culture was behind by about fifty-five years: women were abused and weren't supposed to have an intellectual thought; children were taken out to the woodshed with a switch or belt; and outsiders weren't welcome. Having been born in the Kentucky, I thought I had come home. It only took a month after moving onto the property to shatter that dream.

We walked slowly around the inside of the hospital, reading bulletins, not talking, just holding hands. When we went back to the ward, we stayed in the visitors' lounge until we ran out of things to talk about.

Jim kissed me. "Do you need anything?" He didn't want to leave; he didn't want to stay, either.

"No. I don't need anything." He looked so lost. "I love you."

"I love you, too." His shoulders slumped.

"You know, none of this is your fault. You just married someone with a past that stayed hidden until now." I felt sorry for him.

"I know. Barb told me. It's just that it's so sudden and…so weird. I don't know what to do or say."

"Just do what you've been doing. We'll get through this." It hit me hard in that moment that I hadn't shared much of myself with him in the nearly forty years we had been married; I had behaved more like a soft bully. When we were first married, he was the one who had set the pace of our lives. Somewhere, somehow we traded roles, and I stared at him now like I was seeing him for the first time.

"Do you have any more surprises?" He chuckled.

That was Jim for you. The only way he could cope most times was with humor.

When I got to my room, my clothes and purse were on my bed. I took a shower and washed my hair and blow-dried it. Looking at my styled, snow-white hair and face with no makeup, I couldn't see that I looked any different, other than more worry lines. Dressed in street clothes, I immediately felt better, yet apprehensive. The doctor telling me I might be leaving on Friday did not sit well. I felt safe here, embraced, my needs met by smiling people. Walking out of the room with my book, I heard the TV as the door to the lounge closed. *I guess this time is as good as any to get out into public.*

Three men were in the lounge. I cautiously moved toward the one vacant chair and sat down.

"It's about time you came outta your room." The man who spoke quickly glanced in my direction before turning back to the TV. "I was going to come down and get you today iffin you was still there." He was in his early thirties.

I looked at the floor instead of at him when I asked, "You were the one in the hall when I came in, weren't you?"

My new shyness didn't make any sense to me. I had always been comfortable in male company, whether they wanted mine or not. This was a dramatic change. I didn't know from where it came or if I was comfortable with it.

"Aw, hell, honey, we all have our bad days. You doin' all right now?" He turned to me, smiling.

He reminded me of a puppy that made friends easily with everyone. "I'm better. Thank you." I couldn't help chuckling, in spite of myself.

"You're welcome." He turned back to the TV.

I stayed in there for another thirty minutes chitchatting with each of them in turn, during which time everyone played musical chairs. They weren't used to having a woman around and walked in and out of the lounge for one reason or another, not sure how to behave. When all the small talk was done, the men went back to watching their action movie. I left and went back to my quiet room.

The afternoon was filled with more talk sessions and a movie about the different types of medication offered for PTSD victims. The silence in the group was further proof that the men weren't accustomed to women on the ward—until I started asking questions. Some of them nodded their heads, indicating they had the same questions. One of them even grinned at me, a crusty old man with wild hair and a deep, gravely voice.

I had asked if I would still have strange dreams with the medication and would I be able to sleep without waking up several times during the night.

"If you go to sleep at all." It was the wild-haired man.

"Your mind doesn't stop," I responded.

He nodded his head.

"When you wake up, you don't feel rested."

He nodded his head.

"Dreams are violent?"

Again, he nodded.

"After lying there for a while and sleep doesn't come…"

"…you go and fix yourself a drink," he whispered, still nodding his head.

"You, too?" *I thought I was the only one.*

"You're not the only one, ma'am. It happens to all of us." When he had first sat down in his chair, he leaned a little to his right. Not moving in his chair, he responded while appearing to lean against an invisible pole.

I looked to the facilitator. "Is it true these are the symptoms of PTSD?"

"Yes."

"I've had them for years," I blurted out in a high-pitched voice. "Why did this flashback come now?" I was hoping against hope. This was the same question I had asked of everyone.

"I don't know," she responded in a voice filled with pity.

No one knew.

Thursday, the psychiatrist came into my quiet room with the PA and told me I was going home the next day. I looked at him and said, "You know, it's not nice out there." I nodded toward the outside world. "I feel safe in here."

Leaning against the doorjamb with his hands behind him, the psychiatrist said, "It's a false sense of security."

"Has anything been set up for me?" I was thinking of the rape therapist, Jan Lyndsey.

"We haven't been able to set up anything as yet. We do have an appointment for you with the PTSD Clinic, though. They can set things up for you from there. Is there anything else I can do for you?" He smiled and his eyes weren't searching my thoughts like when I first met him.

I sat quietly while a zillion things went through my head. "No. I do thank you folks for what you've done for me. This whole thing still blows me away, you know. It feels like I'm looking at someone else's life, not mine. But in another way, it answers a few questions and explains a few behaviors, I think." I had been contemplating what I was going to do once I got home again, if it was, indeed, my home. I didn't feel like the same person who created it. *No. I'm not the same person at all.*

"I'll sign the papers today for your release tomorrow. Be sure to call us if you need anything. Okay?" He moved away from the doorjamb and smiled before closing the door.

I go home tomorrow. Home! It sounded odd to my ears. I felt like I had lived a lifetime in the past four days. The hospital had become my home and my stomach knotted up at the idea of leaving.

On Friday, I stopped by the ER looking for the nurse who had checked me in. I spotted her as I passed the same room I had been in. When she saw me, she excused herself and came out into the hall.

"How are you? I've wondered about you." Her smile lit her face.

So humbled by her tender concern, I took a moment for my throat to relax before I responded in a hoarse whisper. "I just wanted to thank you for your kindness when I came in."

"Honey, it's my privilege to serve those who have served. You take care, okay?" She went back into the room. When she sat down again, she waved and smiled.

On the way out, I felt tears on my cheeks. My tears didn't usually flow so freely. I remembered a time not too long ago when I wished I could cry. By the time we got to the car, I was smiling and nearly floating. It was the best I had felt in a long time, and it felt good to be outside.

✻

Meadow Saffron—My best days are gone

I had been home two weeks when I got up one morning and looked into the mirror. A stranger stared back at me. The blue-eyed woman who once wore business suits now wore stained clothing, even though she wasn't working on anything that would stain them. Her hair was uncombed when once upon a time it had been meticulously styled. Her memory had gone from remembering an appointment of six months ago to checking the calendar twice daily to make sure of the day. I gazed at this ugly mess of an unknown, stripped of her beliefs and of nearly all the things that had made her who she was.

I had become someone who didn't know how or what to do from that point with the rest of her life because there was no purpose, no drive. How does someone start over at 60? Where does one start? Do I want what friends I have, and why do I have them? How do I make new friends? Do I want to? It was maddening, frightening. I went through every day the best I could with a husband who was desperately trying his best to comprehend what had happened.

I wondered what I had built the last forty years of my life on. Was it all a lie? Was I the person I thought I knew? More times than I cared to count, people had told me how strong I was, willful even. If I was so strong, how could I have allowed someone to inflict such a heinous act on me? How could I have suppressed it all those years and not have had a clue? If I had suppressed that horror, what else was I suppressing? *No...can't go there, woman. You have enough to deal with.*

I knew I was tired of fighting and of constantly having to prove myself; tired of building our home; tired of my life. Hell, I was just plain tired of hurting on all levels. I had no clue how to find out who I was...am. I had no direction. So I waited. Each day, I sorted through my thoughts thinking perhaps I'd have some answers for the therapist when I saw her in two months. Each day I kept thinking. *When did the breakdown begin? What had caused it?*

Could this or that have been the beginning of my breakdown?

Then, no, that wasn't the beginning.

Could it have been my truck accident in 1999, from which I wasn't expected to survive? After the accident, my taste for alcohol was gone; my desire for cigarettes was gone; and so was my black button. I could get angry, but it didn't stay beyond the moment.

No, not back far enough.

It never occurred to me that all of these events were just small leaks escaping from under a lid that was covering hidden emotions and suppressed memories, where things fermented and brewed until the lid had blown off with my flashback.

Fears being debilitating, I immediately confront them to get rid of them. I never allow an emotion to control me. I'd had control over my emotions my whole life, and to say the flashback had put me in a state of total helplessness was an understatement. Just to be sure I wasn't going to have another *attack*...or explode...or something, I contacted Dr. Andrews, a clinical psychologist who specialized in PTSD.

The rape therapist wasn't available for two months. Meanwhile, I experienced fears, trepidation, and relief—emotions I hadn't experienced in years. I sat at the computer, washed dishes, lay in bed, or just sat in a chair on the porch and cried unprovoked tears. I knew them to be tears caused by those same newly re-experienced emotions. I kept going over the description of the rape I had given to the clinical psychologist.

*

Bill, an NCO, was edgy, nervous, and very short with me. We had not met when he had called me a couple of days earlier. This was our first time together. I was thinking how alike all these men were. But something wasn't right with this one and I couldn't quite put my finger on it.

The room was cast in a yellow glow from both the yellowed lampshades and the nicotine-stained walls. Bill was talking a mile a minute. While he made a whiskey and soda for me, I studied the room's tackiness, with its faded bedspread and green carpet. Motel rooms seemed to be getting cheaper and cheaper. *Like me.* I went into the bathroom. Bill stopped talking. When I came out, he smiled broadly, content with himself.

Taking the proffered drink, I sipped slowly. Bill had undressed and looked unappealing in the dim light. I realized I didn't want to be there. As he moved closer, I noted again that he looked pleased with himself. Odd he should change like that. Like a chameleon. His talking got on my nerves and I told him to wait awhile, that I needed to get in the mood. I took a few more sips of my drink. *Odd taste!* I needed alcohol more and more now. I wondered if I was an alcoholic.

"Hurry up with that drink, damn it. I don't have all night."

I emptied my glass's contents and walked over to Bill. He started to undress me. "Kiss me first, you idiot. You do know how to make out don't you?" I snapped at him.

The room didn't look right, like the walls moved a little on their own. *Christ, what's going on?* I made a movement to push Bill away, but my efforts were clumsy. I didn't even touch him. He looked fuzzy to me as his hands finished undressing me. *No one is that fast.* I watched my hand as it moved in slow motion in an effort to push him away again. He laughed out loud.

"Turn around, bitch. This is all you women are good for you know." He spun me around like a rag doll. *Where in the hell are my muscles?* The room swam.

He snarled, "Bend over, you fucking whore," while roughly shoving my shoulders down, forcing my head toward the floor. *My*

God, I can't fight back. Please, God, help me! Bill gripped me around my hips, and I heard him panting as he struggled to walk/shuffle me to the wall. *He's going to rape me…my God, what is he shoving in?* I tried to struggle. My brain fought with everything it had, but my body refused to move or make a sound. *Surely, that's not him.*

"I'm not ready," I wanted to scream, but nothing came out of my mouth. All I could do was fight for my breath. The carpet faded away. *Please stop, the pain is too much.* He kept shoving it in and out. *My God, it hurts.* I passed out.

Sounds at the door caused me to open my eyes slowly. The noise was loud and hurt my head. God, I hurt…and I was cold! Looking down over my naked body, I saw blood. *Is that my blood?* There was so much of it, dried on my legs, on the carpet, and on the bed. So much blood!

Someone kicked the door in. *It's Ron. Oh God Ron, please help me.* I didn't know if my tears were tears of relief or tears for the great pain in my body.

Ron sobbed. "Lady, are you all right? Answer me. Please."

I couldn't speak. I heard him, but I felt like I was a million miles away. BG placed a blanket over me and carried me, while making comforting cooing sounds. He looked a little familiar, but I found it very hard to open my eyes.

"Is she going to be all right, Ron?" BG asked.

"I don't know. There's so much blood!"

"Yeah, like he cut her open or something."

✻

My first visit with the clinical psychologist was for the intake, and I wrote about the flashback before the second visit. I confessed to feeling better and didn't see him again. My dreams soon indicated there were other flashbacks waiting to come forth, and I crammed them down. I also lived in what I later learned was termed 'a constant state of hypervigilance.'

*

Pimpernel—Change

When the therapist came out of the receptionist's office, she looked at me and smiled. My heart softened, but the butterflies stayed in their space, fluttering their wings slowly. "Hello, I'm Jan. You're Lady?"

Like there's another female in the waiting area!

"Yes," I said, almost in a whisper.

Speak up woman. You're not a mouse. Though I felt like one and wished I were one.

"Follow me, please."

Her voice indicated her gentleness, so I meekly followed my new master like a newborn kitten.

There was plenty of space in the office; a need for space around me was something else I had added to my new list of personal needs. I sat in a chair, liking the idea of it being the close to the door and against the wall.

She took a moment to glance through the file. "When they first called me, my schedule wouldn't allow me to come and visit you. I'm sorry about that."

Her looking me straight in the eye embraced me somehow, and the muscles across my shoulders relaxed a little. "Everything in its time, I guess. I was scared of another attack, so I contacted a clinical psychologist. He had me write an account of the rape." I knew I was talking fast, but I sped on. "I didn't seem to need him after the second visit. But something has happened and I don't understand what's going on. Actually, I don't understand any of this." Nervous and scared, I blurted out, "How can someone suppress this kind of horror for over forty years?" I took a deep breath. *Please tell me. I'm going nuts here.*

She leaned forward on one elbow, and slightly toward me, creating a sense of intimacy. "A trauma can be so severe that we block it out of our memory. Sometimes, it's the only way we can survive the trauma."

"If I suppressed that one, could I be suppressing more of them?" I held my breath.

"Yes. You're a very strong woman, Lady. You'd have to be to have suppressed this for as long as you have."

"I look in the mirror and I don't know who I am. I feel like I've built the last forty years on a lie. How do I correct that? I mean, where do I go from here?" *Girlfriend, I need a magic pill here. I need something instant, like magical words to put the pieces back into place.*

"We can't erase the last forty years. From what you've indicated in your records, you're educated, though you've held many jobs.

What we need to do is to look at what has happened, get through it the best we can and—"

"We?" I couldn't help but smile at her.

"Yes, we." She smiled back.

I had always stood alone. Since leaving the VA hospital I had done nothing except immerse myself in retrospection, trying my best to bring some kind of sense or semblance of order to my life. There was a change within me that didn't click with anything I had read or experienced.

I had been a spiritual counselor since I was twenty-one but I had never encountered anything with any of my clients, except for the vets, that compared with what I was going through. I never hung out a shingle and was never formally trained, but I had a gift for seeing into other people's situations, getting to the source of their problem, and giving solutions. That is, everyone's but my own. My abilities had helped me understand other people and, in the workforce, helped me put coworkers into positions that best suited their talents. My strength also wouldn't allow anyone to bowl me over, which, in some respects, instilled a little fear in some of my coworkers.

"Do you have a copy of what you wrote for your clinical psychologist?"

I reached into my purse and handed her the folded sheets of paper.

She asked, "Would you like this back, or should I make it part of your file?"

I was surprised. "I have a choice of what goes into my file?"

"Yes, to a point. If you intend harm to someone, by law, they have the right to know if their life is threatened."

I was told that in the ER. "Just read it and give it back to me. I'm not comfortable having it loose in some folder."

"Okay! " She started reading then startled me out of my wayward thoughts when she asked, "Do you wish to elaborate on this?"

"Elaborate?"

"Do you want to add to it?"

"No. The truth is, I still wonder if I'm not looking into someone else's life. The whole scenario explains a few things, but I have questions about it being PTSD." It felt good to talk about it. Hell! It felt good to put a finger on it. "What is it exactly? I thought it only pertained to war experiences." I heard a small whine in my voice and was aggravated with myself.

"Not at all. Those who have been abused, doctors, policemen, ER personnel, and anyone who has dealt with death can be a victim of PTSD."

I latched onto that word. "Jan, that's exactly how I feel: a victim. What am I supposed to do with this thing? How do I deal with it?"

"That's why you're here. We'll use each session to deal with your needs as they arise, and to talk about what you need to talk about until you're comfortable. There's no cure for PTSD because we can't cut out our memories. But you can learn to deal with them."

There were only a few minutes left in the session, so we made appointments for every two weeks, which was all her schedule would allow.

It was like a puff of wind blew away those two weeks of time in between. We discussed things in each session, and I appeared to get better. However, the more I relaxed, the more I felt something was hidden in the recesses of my mind, crouching in the dark, just waiting for me to relax so it could pounce.

I felt better on some levels after each session, but I also felt the encroachment of *that thing*. I tensed and became even more hypervigilant. The sessions with Jan had started in November, about three months after I got out of the hospital. Feeling I could handle things on my own by then, I stopped seeing her in February, with the understanding I could see her if I needed it.

Things at home were better. I no longer needed alcohol. I no longer jumped on Jim for everything he did or said. He sighed with relief but he, too, acted as though he expected me to blow up or suddenly turn on him. He tried his level best to be sure I was comfortable. Sometimes, his tiptoeing around me got on my nerves, that and his constantly asking me if I was okay.

I still didn't feel comfortable in my "new shoes," as I referred to my life after the hospital. Things had changed so much. I had changed and could barely keep up. Jan couldn't tell me what triggered the flashback. As I slowly let go of my obsession about wanting to know what triggered it, I began to wonder more about what had caused me to suppress the memories.

If I'm so strong, why didn't I just tell Bill to back off? Why did I go with him? And why didn't I listen to my instincts about him and the situation?

As always, I needed to know. I had to understand why my psyche suppressed the memories in the first place. I thought I'd always stood strong; stood up to my battles; fought the good fight in protecting myself. Yet, something kept niggling at me, like a finger scratching on the inner wall of my brain, but it remained elusive.

In April, I had my compensation and payment appointment, better known as a C & P. I didn't understand what the appointment was and later learned it was the session that determined the percentage of disability payment. The female psychologist was nice and I liked her at first, but her questions dredged up memories like a backhoe digging up garbage, one shovelful at a time. I became agitated, ready to cuss her out.

"What do you mean, 'How did I feel about the rape?' I wanted to castrate the bastard." *Stupid bitch!*

She turned her chair toward me and asked, "Have you had any miscarriages?"

Surprised by her question, I responded, "Yes, all of them.

"How many was that?"

"Six."

She turned back to her computer and started typing. I sat there, dumbfounded, in the quiet room. The silence soon rang with each click of the keyboard. Each tap clicked louder and louder until each click tapped my skin like a tiny electric shock.

What do the deaths of six babies have to do with anything? Why is that important?

The silence stretched on as my chest squeezed my breath, preventing it from leaving my body except in a slow, narrow stream. My thought processes stopped after slogging through a quagmire. Then a dark, forbidden, lone thought crept in like a deadly shadow in front of my mental screen, forcing me to look at it. I tried to push it away, but I was held immobile in the chair.

Please, God. Have I not been punished enough?

After that, the psychologist didn't ask too much about the flashback, but asked about my childhood and my teenage years. I managed to answer her questions, but my throat burned with bile drawn up from my stomach. The nausea wouldn't pass and stayed with me during the drive home.

I was pregnant when I transferred to the new base. The blood in my flashback wasn't all from an internal injury. The clinical psychologist had told me there were men out there with very large penises. Bill had forced my miscarriage.

I knew psychological pregnancies existed. *Can there be such a thing as psychological miscarriages?* My brain reached out and touched that dark, forbidding shadow, dragging it into the light.

I killed my babies.

✻

Ragweed—Courage

The ceiling mirror reflected my naked body on the bed. Holding a bowie knife, a naked a man stood beside the bed. He deftly encircled my left nipple with the tip of the blade, drawing droplets of blood. "Suck it baby, or I cut off the nipple."

The odor of his penis smelling like rotting fish made my stomach flip over and the bile rose into my throat.

I can give him a blow job then throw up, or I can spend the next several weeks healing from my nipple being sewn on.

Jerking upright to a sitting position, I felt sick to my stomach and cold. Looking over at Jim, I saw most of the covers were on him.

"Are you all right," he asked, sitting up, wide awake.

"Yes. I'm going to get up for a while. You go back to sleep," I responded as I took my half of the covers and tugged them over my side of the bed. I didn't want to alarm him. He got on my nerves enough already, watching me as though I would momentarily change into The Hulk.

Putting on my robe in the darkness, I felt my hands shake while tying the belt. The nightmare stayed with me. I couldn't shake it. *That couldn't have been me in that bed, casually making that kind of choice. No, that was someone else in that bed.* I didn't want it to be me, but I knew it was.

I also knew this to be the thing that had crouched in the dark corners of my mind since the flashback. *How could I have become so emotionally numb as a human being that I would allow someone to take a knife to me like that? What caused me to get to that point? When did I get to that point?* The clock showed 2 a.m.

I stayed up the rest of the night, too afraid to go back to sleep. *I wonder if that's why I cup my boob?* While lying in bed, I sometimes wrap my left hand around my left breast and use two fingers to softly pinch the nipple. Sometimes, I even wake up with my hand around my breast. This wasn't done for sensual or sexual purposes. I was never in that frame of mind when I did it. At the time I'd sense it to be a quick gesture to make sure everything was there and all right, though, I never understood why I had to check.

At first, I was embarrassed when I caught myself doing it. But, after awhile, the gesture was so automatic I rarely gave it a thought. There were occasions when I'd look down at my hand and wonder why I did it. Now, I'm convinced it was an unconscious reflex. The mirrors on the ceiling in the hotel room also explained why I was uncomfortable with mirrors.

My nightmares were bad, but, so help me, my waking hours

weren't much better. There were times, if I stood still long enough, I'd hear strange noises: the clinking of filled drinking glasses; soft voices, laughing; deep voices of men in a huddle. The voices didn't talk directly to me, but I began to wonder if I was schizophrenic. I sat at my computer for long hours playing FreeCell game or Solitaire, or searching the Internet, anything to quiet and divert my thoughts.

Tears, waiting just behind my eyelids for a glance or a word of any kind came too easily, too many, and too spontaneously. Sketchy, fragmented memories affected my short-term memory, because I used so much mental energy trying to piece them together. There were times I couldn't remember what I had been told five minutes before and, feeling foolish, wouldn't ask the person to repeat what was said. The memory fragments either took up a large space in my brain, or created a great space. When I said what I thought was in my mind, the information came out in fragments, or not precisely the way I meant it to come out.

Crowds became a real problem. If I walked into a room I'd immediately search for all the exits, should I get trapped for some reason. I tolerated loud noises for a while, but eventually I'd have to leave the room when the noise became a loud buzz or a drone in my head, setting my nerves on edge and sometimes giving me a headache. I had always jumped at sudden noises. Now, tiny, sometimes imagined, noises made me jerk, always edgy.

And sensitive! I was beyond it, sometimes even paranoid. *What did they mean by that? What do they want from me? What do they want me to do? What do they want in return?* My brothers had teased me about being gullible when, in fact, I had simply trusted everyone. I'd always searched for that someone in whom I could place my confidence. Trust was now a real issue. I even began questioning my trust in Jim. Could I believe everything he told me?

I was afraid to go to bed. Though my antidepressant medication helped me to sleep, it didn't assuage my fear of dreams. I moved around in the daylight, but was afraid that anything I did or said would bring on another flashback. I kept away from people as much as I could.

I couldn't figure out why I was so angry after we moved to Tennessee, to a small community hidden away in a big crevice of the mountains south of the Kentucky border. But within a very short time after moving, I became bitchy, moody, angry, and snapped at the littlest thing. Truth be known, I don't know how Jim stayed with me for so long without really losing it.

There were times I sat in as counselor to my thoughts, asking myself questions and trying to answer them. One summer day, sitting on the swing looking at our killer view of the mountains, the answer to one question came out of nowhere and hit the inside of my head like a hard slap. Every man who had ever sexually abused me was from the south, and nearly all had Southern accents. My first step father, all the men where I was stationed, and those who had abused me the worst were from the south.

Upon hearing Southern accents on a daily basis, I acted out in anger. Not knowing why I was so angry, I had sought out every possible venue: drinking, Marijuana, four-wheeling with the guys, bar hopping, looking for God knows what.

A new kind of anger pervaded my senses. It wasn't deep anger at the world, but anger at myself for having been so stupid and gullible. But the anger didn't stay with me. I'm sure it was the combination of the medication, which kept me feeling ill, and the fact that I just couldn't hold onto anger since the truck accident. I'm convinced the accident in '99 actually took away my black button

As hard as it was on my ego, I called Jan for an appointment.

✻

"What's going on?" she asked after we settled into our seats.

"I wish I knew," and went on to explain the nightmare, my awareness of how I had acted out my anger, jumping at the noises, and the voices. "Why do these memories keep coming up and why were they suppressed in the first place? I have other not-so-nice memories, but they stay where they belong."

Should I tell her about the new one trying to come through?

"About two or three years ago it was discovered that memories can come from two parts of our brain: one part is for the visual; the other is for the senses. We smell cinnamon and we have fond memories of apple pie or of our mothers or grandmothers baking. If it's a traumatic memory and comes back as a flashback, then it comes from both parts of the brain. The psyche will suppress it because it was too much to handle at the time. Years will have passed and the memory will still be suppressed, but our bodies can sometimes create behaviors that will reflect that trauma. What you're experiencing is not abnormal."

"I've been allowing these memories to come forward. You know, owning them. But it's hard." My breathing felt laborious. Sometimes the memories even tried to encroach on my conversations.

"That's brave of you."

"What do you mean brave of me?" *That was a hell of a statement to make.* "This isn't something I want to do."

"You don't have to 'own them,' as you put it."

I sat for a minute struggling to digest what she said. I had always felt I had to be responsible for my own actions. That I had to....

Jan interrupted with, "You didn't ask for this, Lady. You were slipped a Mickey then raped. The flashback is yours, but you don't have to keep remembering it."

Feeling foolish, I looked down at my feet. "Okay."

During the drive home, my mind rehashed what we had discussed. What Jan had put into words regarding our senses being part of the trauma helped me to understand what I had already intuited. None of my clients could remember a trauma without first relating which of the five senses triggered the memory of that trauma.

With me, I knew my insecurities and ineptness had stemmed from my stepfather raping me and seeing and tasting my own blood. My low self-esteem had nurtured these elements throughout my childhood when I believed others when they told me I was stupid. My intuition, when working with our foster children, further attested there was a beginning basis for our pain. Our fears didn't come out of thin air and something had to either create or nurture them.

✻

Magnolia—Perseverance

I again asked for a book explaining why and how I got to the point of allowing people to abuse me. I thought I had always been strong, but evidently at some point in my life, my self-esteem was as low as some of my clients. Jan recommended the book *I Can't Get Over It*, by Aphrodite Matsakis, PH.D., a specialist in PTSD. In her book she describes how triggers can bring on an adrenaline surge and how this surge can bring on memories, events, nightmares, etc.

When I lost my first baby during the sixth month, an autopsy indicated I had miscarried because of too many male hormones. I can only assume my last miscarriage was due to the same condition; but I'll never now since since the hospital lost both the baby and placenta. Autopsy on the first baby, also six months in the womb, indicated the same thing. The four babies in between were aborted between three and four months into the pregnancy. There's no way of knowing for sure, but I'm certain that every time I became pregnant, my adrenal glands, through my own psyche, secreted excess hormones until a hormone imbalance eventually aborted the baby. I also suspect the subconscious memory of the original rape that aborted my baby was what psychologically triggered my adrenal glands. This was powerful to me for it was absolute proof that the mind can kill.

While trying to create a new life, my sessions with Jan helped me keep my sanity while we walked back through what I felt was a surreal past and connected the dots to my present behaviors. The antidepressant medication kept my spirits up, but it didn't stop my fears: fear of another flashback, new or old; fear of people; and fear of noises. Fears were alien to me; I had not been afraid of anything prior to the original flashback.

I struggled daily with my dilemma of keeping something foreboding pushed to the back of my mind, or allowing it to come forth. I lost interest in my fiber art and my studio collected cob webs. I didn't know what I wanted to do, or even if I wanted to do something. I lost interest in gardening; I used to enjoy playing in the dirt and getting dirty. Spiders in the greenhouse spun their webs, free from intrusion. Looking through the greenhouse window, I often wondered if my memories were pretending they were spiders, intricately weaving their webs with holes and strings going to nowhere, but somehow connecting. Usually, I just sat in my rocker and read, or rather, tried to read; I often just stared off into space.

A few weeks later, I was at the clothesline, hanging up sheets as my mother had taught me, first snapping the cloth out in front of me to shake out as many wrinkles as possible. I froze. My sheets faded as three men came at me, each with a sheet in his hand. Fear nailed my feet to the floor I was now standing on as each man tried to place a sheet over my head and wrap it around my waist.

With the first sheet in place, a fourth person raised my skirt and pulled off my panties. Claustrophobia caused me to panic, and I kicked and thrashed until my foot found a soft spot between a man's legs. The bloodcurdling, male animal scream immobilized everyone. Each sensing his personal vulnerable spot, they released their hold on me for just a fraction of a moment. It was long enough for me to thrash my arms and legs as panic-enforced strength helped me to pull the off sheets and stand up, screaming and grunting between heavy intakes of breath.

When I slapped the last sheet away, I found myself in my own yard and looked around immediately to see if anyone was near. It always took a moment or two to discern in which reality I stood.

God, how I could use a drink!

One day, looking out the kitchen window, I realized I hated where I lived. It was a community of male domination. Women were taught to keep a spotless house; raise children; attend church; and keep their mouths shut, except for what they were told to say. In this place, the men thought a smile was a license to take liberties.

I had been fighting this mentality ever since I had moved to the Clinch Mountains, and right then, wondered if I'd stayed because it was a distraction from what was subconsciously going on inside me. It also gave me an outlet for my anger. I now realized how tired I was of the fight.

"Jim, how would you feel about moving away from here?" It

was hard enough to get him to move from Michigan. But he, too, didn't like the people here.

"I wouldn't be opposed to it."

That's my pessimist; can't even give a straight yes answer.

I felt good about the decision to move, a new place, new faces, a fresh start. It had never worked before, but I prayed with all my heart it would work this time.

By the following spring, we had purchased a nice piece of acreage in the mountains of North Carolina. In our little holler, the ridges felt like strong arms encircling me, protecting me. The mountains exuded and filled me with strength. And the solitude was comforting, quiet, with no traffic noise. The gentle wild animals accepted us and meandered across our lawn to the creek.

Time moved slowly. Listening to the small creek chuckling in its passage over the ancient stones, I was reminded to laugh occasionally. Sitting outside, I allowed the wind to softly woo me, whispering as it caressed my cheeks, making me blush. While driving with the windows open and inhaling the fresh clean air, I occasionally caught a waft of wood smoke from a chimney, feather dusting memories in the forgotten corners of my brain, uncovering images of other cold winters, angel wings in the snow, and childhood giggles under fluffy blankets.

In the year it took us to move into our new home, I had time to talk with the residents. Even though a lot of them were local, there were also a lot of nonlocals from all over the country. Listening to the speech patterns that distinguished the various former geographical locations of the residents of our community, I became aware of a slow dawning that spanned several weeks.

My speech slowed, while in the past it had raced like a freight train. Some folks couldn't understand me because I had spoken so fast.

My foot didn't push the gas pedal as hard, when before I had demonstrated extreme road rage. And I relaxed. There were actually days I didn't do anything and didn't feel guilty if I wasn't doing something productive. There was a time I had to be productive, even when sitting down, and thus had needlework in my hands.

When trying to stop tears from flowing became too much like trying to push water up a wall, I let them flow. I could remember a time when I had prayed for the ability to cry; now I couldn't control the tears. Emotions! My God! When I discovered what some of them were, I realized I hadn't felt them since the rape.

There were times when someone would catch me off guard by evoking a new emotion within me. I'd stand very still, with a blank look on my face, while emotions bounced all over the insides of my body and brain. At the time, not understanding what I was feeling or how to respond to the person standing in front of me, I'd just walk away. I'm certain I left these people very confused or wondering what they had said or done.

On another summer day, while mowing the lawn with our riding mower, I moved into some tall weeds thinking I could mow them down. Backing out of them, a vine with thorns scratched the back of my leg and I cried out in pain. Looking down I saw blood coming from a long, ugly scratch that soon looked more like a deep slit, and I swore. The pain was also increasing.

Pain! The shock of feeling the pain glued my butt to the seat of the mower. Watching the blood flow down my leg, I smiled. As the pain increased, my smile turned into laughter then into tears of joy. For as long as I could remember, I had been unable to feel pain in my legs. The skin could be lying open, the blood clotting or dried, and even then, someone would have to tell me I had been wounded. I never felt pain below my waist…until now. Intuition led me to believe that I had stopped feeling pain in my legs after the sheet incident, when the four men had exposed me from the waist down.

For a few months after the vine scratched me, my legs felt everything. I couldn't even rest my ankle on my knee without both of them throbbing after a few moments. My ankle bracelet came off because I couldn't stand the pressure of a sock pressing the bracelet against my skin. It was like my legs had come alive, and I was feeling every nerve in them. Even creases in the sheets at night woke me. And the wind—It was the first time I felt the wind brush my legs.

I saw Jan for few more sessions before she released me from therapy. We had already discussed the flashback and the few months of abuse that took place afterward. It was during our discussion of my first stepfather making me a victim of incest that a thought reverberated inside of my brain like a ping pong ball bouncing off a wall.

The beginning, you idiot: if you want to know what started a thing you need to go back to the beginning...the very beginning.

*

Dog Rose—Pleasure & pain

I moved into our new home by myself at the end of February; Jim joined me later. Many afternoons, I'd sit outside, listening to the wind blowing in the trees surrounding our home. Our house sits in a bowl embraced by wood-covered ridges on both sides and behind the house, with a front view of a farmhouse down the hill and several mountain ridges farther on. After each trip from the dome, I'd unpack and put the things away. My mind would be still, and so would wander off into the past. When I found myself taking the newly unpacked items out of one place and putting them where they belonged in another, I would just get a chair and sit outside, letting my brain wander where it needed to go.

After I had moved, I went on the Internet and looked up PTSD, as there are no blood tests or x-rays to determine its presence. I found the *Psychiatric News*, October 18, 2002, Volume 37, Number 20, on page 25, that describes the DSM-IV-TR Criteria for post-traumatic stress disorder (PTSD), and it reads:

A. The person has been exposed to a traumatic event in which both of the following were present:

 1. The person experienced, witnessed, or was confronted with an event or events that involved actual or threatened death or serious injury, or a threat to the physical integrity of self or others.
 2. The person's response involved intense fear, helplessness, or horror.

B. The traumatic event is persistently re-experienced in one (or more) of the following ways:

 1. Recurrent and intrusive distressing recollections of the event, including images, thoughts, or perceptions.
 2. Recurrent distressing dreams of the event.
 3. Acting or feeling as if the traumatic event were recurring (includes a sense of reliving the experience, illusions, hallucinations, and disassociative flashback episodes, including those that occur on awakening or when intoxicated).
 4. Intense psychological distress at exposure to internal or external cues that symbolize or resemble an aspect of the traumatic event.
 5. Physiological reactivity on exposure to internal or external cues that symbolize or resemble an aspect of the traumatic event.

C. Persistent avoidance of stimuli associated with the trauma and numbing of general responsiveness (not present before the trauma), as indicated by three (or more) of the following:

1. Efforts to avoid thoughts, feelings, or conversations associated with the trauma.
2. Efforts to avoid activities, places or people that arouse recollections of the trauma.
3. Inability to recall an important aspect of the trauma.
4. Markedly diminished interest or participation in significant activities.
5. Feeling of detachment or estrangement from others.
6. Restricted range of effect (e.g., unable to have loving feelings)
7. Sense of a foreshortened future (e.g., does not expect to have a career, marriage, children, or a normal life span.)

D. Persistent symptoms of increased arousal (not present before the trauma), as indicated by two (or more) of the following:

1. Difficulty falling or staying asleep.
2. Irritability or outbursts of anger.
3. Difficulty concentrating
4. Hyper-vigilance.
5. Exaggerated startle response.

E. Duration of the disturbance (symptoms in Criteria B, C, and D) is more than one month.

F. The disturbance causes clinically significant distress or impairment in social, occupational, or other important areas of functioning.

The above description was far lengthier than that of Dr. Matsakis. I immediately latched onto the word "helplessness." This word resonated with each and every trauma I remembered. Helplessness, in my experience, is not an emotion, but a state of mind, a state of "no control." You have no tools with which to deal with your trauma. No words to express your anger. For a few moments nothing registers. Nothing! The shock is so great there's usually no thought that can penetrate into the psyche when the brain is under such stress. In moments of horrific shock, my psyche imprinted upon my brain, not only the visuals of the scenes, but one or more of my five senses. After this moment of helplessness that lasts for a heartbeat, there's an instinctive reaction to freeze, flee, or fight. My first reaction was to freeze.

I often wondered if, in my youth, I had been given the tools to deal with abuse or traumas, if I would have learned to fight or flee, rather than freeze. I also wondered if low self-esteem caused me to freeze, thinking I didn't deserve any better and, therefore, zoning out during the abuse. In my adult life, it took only an imprinted sense or a word to send me back to the past to virtually relive the trauma.

During any given day I connected with triggers that brought up pleasant memories or what I thought of as something "out of the blue." The smell of Old Spice cologne was one of them. It instantly brought to mind the fat man at the show one Saturday afternoon while I was watching cartoons on the screen. I smelled urine and Old Spice when he sat down next to me. Within a few minutes he started touching me. I told my brother to get up, and we left. While we walked home, I kept looking over my shoulder to see if the smelly man was following us. Every time I smelled Old Spice after that, I would see the fat man in my mind, automatically smelled urine, and looked over my shoulder.

I recall reading somewhere that prey, running from its hunter, may run for a while then just stop, drop to the ground, and wait for its fate—an internal sense telling it there is no escape. If time passes, and by some miracle, the prey is still alive, it will stand up, do a heavy shiver dance to shake off the trauma, then walk away, seemingly none the worse for wear.

Even though we are animal based, humans cannot always shake off life-threatening traumas. I've learned with and through my clients and by my own experiences that the only way we can prevent it from living deep within us is to share it. With no one to share the trauma, and no internal understanding or coping tools gained from a similar experience, I had devised ways of internalizing the trauma as best I could. Unfortunately, "the best I could" wasn't enough and further deepened the pain.

Once I had experienced that state of total helplessness, the elements of fear and ineptness silently programmed themselves into my psyche. At the same time, I subconsciously created and put into place the first ember or spark of anger. Psychologically, I used the mortar of tears and spent emotions to cement into place the first invisible stone wall I thought would protect me, and I spent my life building it. Each instance of a minor or major trauma would resonate with this wall when I remembered or re-experienced a small part of the visual trauma, or if one of my senses was again used to bring on a memory or create a new memory.

With each fear or incident of ineptness experienced after the first trauma, I added a coal of anger to those already smoldering. Had the first trauma (ember) been put out by my somehow dealing with it right after the event, or within a short time, the ember would have died. As it was, it smoldered long enough to spark a fire. This fire of anger intensified with the addition of other embers. This fire eventually turned into rage. This rage became so viable it took on its own entity; *it* was the silent entity that I felt behind me all the time. This was the *it* that stood waiting expectantly, like a stalking, salivating wild beast. My psyche was aware of *it* but couldn't comprehend what *it* was or why the invisible thing felt so real.

Fearing *it* had taught me to stay in front of it, to keep it behind me. This fear, stemming from the raging fire of anger within me, was the basis for my road rage, spiking anger, and sudden shifts of emotions so dramatic that others wondered if I had a split personality when I suddenly turned on them. Anger, for the most part, was the only emotion I felt and it pushed down all others, numbing me. Anger drove me, though it didn't present itself like anger. It made me super efficient so that it took more than one person to replace me whenever I left a job

My mind never shut down, never stopped. It often looked for

different ways to do a thing because the old way was no longer interesting. I quickly became bored with jobs and felt the need to get another one, as different and as challenging as possible.

My counseling others had taught me that anger could create another personality within you, and if allowed to grow, it becomes its own entity. This personality can take on and make strong a certain trait. This trait, growing stronger, will perform certain tasks; i.e., if you're nervous about taking tests or talking back to another, your stronger personality trait will take over these tasks. If the new personality becomes strong enough, it will take over and suppress you. You may not be able to remember what the stronger personality has said or done.

This entity called anger comforted me; it justified my screw-ups; it justified my hurting others; it was true to me and wouldn't turn on me. Sometimes, it forced me to face up to another, giving me a false sense of courage, strength or intellect; it turned me into a bully. The entity had become such a good friend, I abhorred the idea of forcing it to leave. Even though my psyche had created this entity within me, I wasn't aware of its powers until someone or something showed me the behaviors this demon created—each behavior as unique as I was because of my life experiences. Even then, my friend, anger, would convince me the person pointing out the behaviors was wrong.

✻

Sage-Wisdom

My anger was a fire so alive that its excitement wasn't comparable to anything else. I constantly searched for external excitement to equal the exciting fiery anger within me. As all things in the universe, there must be a balance, my psyche sought external means of equalizing the internal self. The term is "self-medicating," and these actions created behavior disorders, sometimes compulsive, like drug/alcohol abuses; surrounding myself with "stuff" because I didn't feel loved; excess food intake; spending money; sex for the euphoric sensation during climax; racing anything on wheels; any perilous act that put me at risk for that ultimate thrill, my need to defy.

Occasionally, I recalled what an adult advocate said one time about an abused woman. The woman was asked why she left a relationship with a man who loved her, gave her a good home, and supported her and her children. She responded, "It was too boring."

The key word being *boring*. She was unaware of the fire within her because the fire burns very quietly, its intensity very cold.

I now understand that the woman was only aware of the external need to be excited. Hence, she provoked a fight that brought on abuse followed by the honeymoon period; the stage where the abuser asks for forgiveness and acts the lover. The excitement of the abuse, the sex that follows, sometimes followed by alcohol or something to smoke as a sense of celebration, is what the woman sought. For a while, she was satisfied…but only for a while. The fire needs the continual external fuel.

I began to understand how and why abusers were a product of abuse. They, too, have this internal fire that must be sated. They express their anger and need for control with their fists, verbal abuse, or with mind games. In nearly all instances, since the abuser has no control over what is going on within himself, he will try to control his spouse's activities by keeping her friends at a distance, if not cutting her off completely. He'll tell her he can take her kids because she's an unfit mother, or he'll abuse a child to show her his power and how far he'll go with it. He'll use her ignorance or ineptness to any degree that will empower him.

When the same adult advocate asked an abuser what it was about a woman that told him he could abuse her, he replied that he could watch a woman walk across the street and know if he could abuse her. He named four traits:

1. Rounded or sloped shoulders—the fire is a great burden. This trait is the most prevalent of all the body languages for those with low self-esteem.

2. They will walk with small steps, will not step out.
3. There is very little eye contact—the lack of courage to "face" another. This one was different for me. I held eye contact. But others don't want someone to think they are being confronted and they don't want to invite a confrontation.
4. They continually apologize by starting their sentences with "I'm sorry...." This can also be seen in body language.

I've discovered through my own body language, and that of some of my clients, behavior patterns stemming from a state of helplessness, in both men and women. From the first experience of having no control, control became an obsession—a lot of times over-powering anything else. My body language and the psychological reasons involved with my anger mirrored others I have witnessed in my various careers, and in those I have counseled.

1. Rapid and/or constant speech—fear of hearing the embers crackle or a spark would burn me if I stopped; the need to psychologically keep it a good distance in front of it, so I ran with my speech.
2. The need to dominate the conversation or be the center of attention—I felt like I was floundering and didn't want to drown, get lost, or be ignored.
3. My hands flew, usually in the faces of others, as I spoke. Though I enjoyed the attention, low self-esteem deemed me unworthy, so I felt the need to push people away.
4. Arms folded across the chest—the protective stance. This trait is prevalent with everyone if they are discussing

something sensitive to themselves, or if they fear being hurt. It is a move to protect the heart. This was also my way of saying, "No matter what you say...." Much like standing in defiance with my hands on my hips. When my hair was long, I would move my head to move the hair out of the way or out of my face. This is similar to a mental karate stance. Someone preparing themselves for defense.

5. I became efficient, worked overtime hours to do what I thought others could not or would not do to my satisfaction. I was an overachiever, doing the work of two or more people. Work was also a distraction. I never wanted accolades, but they would sometimes spur me on.
6. I was so driven, I strongly lead the office or group or created a cause to which I could give my energy, usually my all. This gave me my purpose in life.
7. All of my careers were in a field helping others. I couldn't do anything for myself, so I did for others. I guess I was also looking for answers, especially if I was aware of something amiss in my own character.

✻

I was so focused and driven that I sometimes wore blinders to everything and everyone in my immediate surroundings. This focused drive masked or shut down other emotions, enabling me to live on a day-to-day basis. "Living a life of quiet desperation" is an apt description. I'd bounce from job to snack, to phone, to snack, then maybe to just a small glass of wine, or to outrageous sex, then the next day, perhaps, to another job.

When my anger spiked, I might say or do something to hurt another. Upon hearing what I had just said or seeing what I had just done, I'd become contrite and apologize profusely and try to make up for it. Not understanding what was going on with my mood swings and acid tongue, I never kept friends. Eventually it was better to be left alone than to go through the hassle of forming a relationship only to shatter it. If folks were uncomfortable with me—oh well.

My internal fire became a friend so familiar that it inspired me to build a stronger wall. This inspiration became so strong, so invasive, the distraction of it caused me to mishear or miss entirely what was said or not see what was done. I fed on it. Indeed, it became my food, my shield, the anger became the very reason I got out of bed in the morning. It made me feel alive. It kept me alive.

The one exception was when I tried to commit suicide while in the Navy. The fire had gone out and there was no longer a reason to live. I had reached a point the anger had taken over my life, and I was out of control. There was no one there; I was alone in my decision. There was no longer a reason to live because my fire had burned itself out.

I can honestly relate two facts. If someone is talking about committing suicide, it is a cry from the individual saying, "Please, help me before I do this thing." If another listens and does something, the person will probably not go through with the suicide. Not always, though.

Fact two, if the person doesn't speak to anyone about what

they're internalizing, they will proceed. Or they have probably already put out their internal fire, their reason to live, and have made plans. Sometimes those plans take awhile, other times the suicide is a spontaneous decision. In any case, the fire is no longer burning because hopelessness has put out the flames; hopelessness was what had put out mine. Hearing the word *family* several times while I was standing by the river rekindled a small spark within me. The bus ride home was a lull between two storms. One fire having died, another was rekindled by more emotional and mental abuse.

The positive side to this internal rage was its ability to thrust me into creativity. I'd go into my studio and create something. In my fifties, I was in the gym working out and rediscovered what moving the body does for the brain. I even trained for the senior competitions in racket ball. I realized that I wasn't working for training purposes, but, rather, to get out excess anger. I recognized my anger, but didn't understand from where it came or why it was there.

I remember reading somewhere that some of the most talented people in history have been severely abused in their childhood.

*

Olive Branch—Peace

A few days after moving into our North Carolina home, I checked out the local library. The librarian asked if I wanted to join the local book club. Intrigued, I joyfully agreed; this would be my first group gathering since my stay in the VA hospital. Coffee klatches were never my forte. As a career woman I had no tolerance for recipe trading, gossip swapping, or rug rats' stories. I had had enough of that in my youth.

I walked into the book club meeting, held in a beautiful log home, scared, legs weak, and not knowing anyone except the three I had met in the library. I didn't know what to expect, but it wasn't a room full of intelligent women. The situation also reminded me that I lacked social graces. I had been so busy surviving and working in the male business world, I rarely sat down to have true conversations, especially with other women.

I later learned there had been twenty-three educated women out of twenty-five attending. I felt the power in the room and, at the time, honestly felt I was out of my element. What was very significant was I noted that I had changed into someone totally unlike the woman I had been before the flashback. I had once been an extrovert, and now I was an introvert. I preferred solitude to noise and crowds.

The facilitator of the book club suggested each woman, if she was comfortable with the idea, to write why she came to the community. When I wrote my piece and emailed it out, I was invited to join a writer's club led by Sophia, whom I had also met at the book club. Curious, I attended the writer's club meeting, but was very guarded.

Sophia, an ex-nun, has red hair and soft, angelic qualities. Not that I had ever met an angel, but she certainly embodied gentleness with a quiet demeanor. Without saying a word she reminded me of how course and crude both I and my life had been. I asked if I could write my book and use the members of the writer's club for feedback. Everyone in the club agreed, but within of couple months I withdrew it. I realized I needed to journal my life as my clients did and to do it with only one listener. So Sophia and I continued to meet on a regular basis. I didn't know it at the time, but I actually channeled most my life. I had forgotten so much. It was similar to relating what I saw on a movie screen, but in a monotone voice.

With Sophia, I went back to the original trauma in my childhood using the same tools I used with my clients. She, too, understood that a universal balance must be maintained in any given situation for anyone to remain healthy. If one has been traumatized, healing comes from gentleness and compassion, not further traumatizing through shouting, pointing a finger, or even demeaning the abuser. One faces the original trauma by using the same elements that imprinted it on the psyche, by bringing it out on paper and looking at it. This imprints the trauma in reverse. The senses of touch, sight, and hearing are used when reading it aloud.

I became the client of this quiet, nonjudgmental woman who embraced me when I needed a hug; allowed me to cry without saying "poor thing," and listened to my voice with such rapt attention I sometimes fidgeted. She also used the one important tool I used with my clients—touch. Appropriate, affectionate touch is an element missing in most children's lives, especially those who have been abused.

I experienced firsthand what my clients had gone through. Trauma imbedded itself into my psyche, and it was only in the sharing that I could let it go. If the trauma wasn't shared, the psyche nurtured it, strengthened it and allowed it to build a wall, thinking it would protect itself and me. Trauma had used one or more of my senses to imprint itself. It had always taken a sound, a smell, or a touch to conjure up a memory.

Within several weeks of journaling, my heart lightened when good memories of my youth and teen years moved up through my mental quagmire, and I regained the small joys, long forgotten. The anger I had held onto most of my life had kept them pushed down.

Going back to that first remembered hurt was not an easy thing to do. People have often told me how it takes courage to go back and relive the past. But, truth be known, I think it took more courage to think about it and make the choice. Usually, once people make up their minds to do a thing, it's just a matter of following through. But that's me. Knowing the memories were just memories helped a great deal; no one from the past could hurt me. I viewed the memories of the incidents and events from the outside with a third-party perspective.

The reason I wanted to go back to the beginning was to understand how and why the abuse affected me as it did. Journaling my life showed me why I had made my choices. The decisions I had made through the forty years after the rape were based on that incident in ways that created a wall between me and the outside world. Once the psyche took in the experience of the military rape, it cut off my emotions to keep from feeling. I understood the need to not feel was necessary to survive in a world of daily hurts.

Had the military rape been my first trauma, it wouldn't have impacted my psyche as deeply. My first trauma was my first stepfather raping me when I was seven years old then my family denying it. Since it wasn't dealt with in some manner, it became the foundation on which all other feelings of insecurity and ineptness attached themselves. Each negative emotion felt, displayed in public, and laughed at or used to make me feel stupid or silly, was another stone laid upon that foundation.

I shared a letter with Jan I had written to say good bye to my six babies. In it I apologized to them as I expressed my thoughts on what I thought each of their personalities might have been. When I shared the letter aloud at home, it had no effect. But when I read aloud to Jan about losing my four sons and two daughters, I cried.

Feeling the release, I understood more about how the psyche worked. Up until then, I could only intuit for my clients.

In the process of sharing my story with Sophia, I began cleaning up the little residuals of pain and anger my psyche had over the years. I learned who I was and why I made the choices I had made. I saw what took place in my life that allowed me to maintain a status quo at a time when my ego and pain wanted to just chuck it all. I know who I am today and where I am going. I have learned that when you process all the anger and all the negative attributes attached to that anger and pain, there is only one element left. Love!

I can honestly say, though I don't like them and despise what they did, I have compassion for the men who hurt me. I will not allow another to abuse me, but I can look back at them now and know from where they came; understand they were hurting and not always in command of their choices; and that most of their choices stemmed from their own traumatized psyches. I just happened to be in their path.

I now understand how a trauma, isolated within us, gains strength. Once it is shared, it no longer has a foundation on which to build. When we face the original hurt, we actually crack the foundation to which all other hurts, pains, and traumas have attached their tentacles, each turning into a stone placed on the foundation. Every time we share a connecting dot to that trauma, we lose a stone in the wall, as the trauma loses its control over our lives. With some of my clients, just looking at the original hurt was enough.

If we start with the present day and work our way back to the trauma, it won't make sense. But if we start with the first trauma and come forward, we can connect nearly all major decisions, feelings of ineptness, and insecurities. We can see how we created our life based on that first trauma and not only how we came to be who we are, but why. Only through understanding what little insecurities or affirmations of pain had done to me and how I had nurtured them, I could rid myself of their stranglehold.

Things I had intuited before now made sense. All negative feelings we feel about ourselves are based on a trauma in our youth, and how low our self-esteem will be is determined by how small or large the trauma, and how it was handled at the time. How much love and affection we have in our lives will also determine how much the trauma affects us. It stands to reason that if there is love and affection, we will usually have an outlet for hurtful events that take place. At the very least there would be someone with whom to share it.

We can deal with trauma by journaling our lives back to our youth. Coming forward from the original hurt, we can see how we made our decisions based on how we were feeling and what we felt we needed to protect ourselves. Once we see how everything connects back, most, if not all, negative aspects of low self-esteem fade away as the psyche heals itself. We need to remember here that the psyche is also looked upon as the ego. Once the ego sees how it had to protect itself, it lets go in the face of new strength based on an understanding.

Walking the same path as my clients, I, too, fell within the same perimeters of the time frame and experienced the same behavior patterns humans travel through when healing. When hurts are shared by bringing them into the light, they dissipate. Hurts only grow in the darkness. As they dissipate, the ego/psyche grieves its loss much the same as we grieve a death. This is part of the healing. The behavior pattern is as unique as the individual and will follow the Five Stages of Grief (as written by Elizabeth Kubler-Ross); though not all may be experienced, or experienced in the order given.

1. **Denial**—"This can't be happening to me,"
2. **Anger**—"Why me?"
3. **Bargaining**—begging, wishing.
4. **Depression**—overwhelming feelings of hopelessness, frustration, bitterness, self-pity, mourning, and lack of control. The need to sleep.
5. **Acceptance**—there is a difference between resignation and acceptance.

I refer to this grieving/healing period as *standing in the rain*, or *fallout*, which starts after sharing the initial trauma. These terms defined what I needed to do while my psyche healed itself. I gave my psyche time to heal while my body reacted to its releasing. I had always stressed to my clients that this process can't be rushed; let the psyche do its thing, at its own pace. Sometimes I had to repeat a sharing, especially the original hurt, in order to allow my brain to digest the idea that I no longer wanted to hold onto it. There were times I had to approach it from different angles to get a different perspective. I also knew I might have to experience the five stages of grief on many different levels and depths, depending on how my psyche nurtured the trauma.

When the flashback hit me, I had no choice but to go back and look at my past. In retrospect, I guess I also got angry when I heard my clients say (which they have, by the way), "Healer, heal thyself."

In July, 2006, I had heart surgery. The night before the surgery, I explained to the surgeon that I needed someone in the recovery room with me to tell me I was, in fact, in the hospital and not somewhere else. That if I awoke with something the size of a penis in my mouth and my hands were restrained, I would react. And the last time I *reacted*, my blood pressure shot up to 200 over 140.

When I came to in recovery, the lighting, along with my lying prone and naked on a bed, started a flashback. I attempted to fend off the attacker with my hands and was utterly stunned to find them free. The shock of seeing my hands through a vision, which was just beginning to change realities, was enough. The flashback did not continue because I stopped it. Previously, I would have suppressed my reaction or suffered through it. In that moment, I knew two things: one, I now had control; two, the doctor had honored me by honoring my request of allowing my hands to be free. I understood the position in which he had placed himself when he made that choice. I pray the written message I later sent to him was enough to let him know the blessed gift of freedom he had given me.

When I came home from the hospital four days after the bypass surgery, I was still on pain pills. I didn't know which was worse, the pain from surgery or the side effects of the pain meds. My friends came over with gifts. One friend's husband performed a ceremony while his wife anointed me with the same precious oils her friends used to anoint her. During the ceremony, another friend contributed her gift by anointing me with holy water her friends and her husband's friends had gathered from all the sacred wells of the world as wedding gifts.

I was also informed after the ceremony that food arrangements had been made by the book club, and that I need not worry about cooking for a while, or about anything else I might require. My husband would also be looked after, as necessary. This loving care lasted for nearly a month, so blessed was I.

I had known for many months that, for the first time in my life, I was in a community of people who embraced me for me. In their quiet way, they let me know they understood without details being given because details weren't needed. There were nights, before my surgery, I cried silent tears of joy while in bed, wondering at my many blessings and knowing I had been placed in my new home for a reason.

That night while lying in bed, I cried for a different reason. I hurt so badly from physical pain and discomfort. It took awhile for my medicated brain to realize the impact of the moment. I was crying for physical pain. *My* physical pain! Not someone else's! My pain! I had not cried for physical pain since my stepfather tried to penetrate me when I was seven years old. When this revelation finally sank in, I cried again, but this time for joy. The words *fifty-five years* kept repeating over and over in my head, until it became a mantra. I spent more than an hour crying that night for both pain and for joy because I knew I had finally processed my original trauma. The mantra lulled me to sleep.

The next morning, I laid my pain pills aside to give them back to my doctor. I didn't need them anymore.

Dealing with PTSD

I have described what a flashback is and what it takes to trigger one. But as you may be aware, an abuse victim is not the only one who can become a PTSD victim.

A soldier in uniform is on foreign ground in a hostile country. From the time he steps foot on that ground, he's on alert, his adrenaline runs on high unless he's sleeping—and I'll wager it's with one eye open. He's ordered out on patrol and knows his buddies have been killed by gun fire coming from any direction. He watches everyone and everything, his chest tightening while he prays his next step isn't on a land mine. He goes to bed hoping he wakes up in it.

A police cruiser hails a vehicle over to the side of the road. You will notice that officers no longer stand in front of the driver's side window, but rather to the back of and behind the driver's window and, therefore, out of the driver's line of vision, exposing as little of their torsos as possible.

A plain-clothes cop shared with me, "When I was on the road, as soon as I turned off my cruiser and got out, my adrenaline started pumping. I never knew what I was going to come up against in that vehicle. I walked to the vehicle at a pace that gave me time to prepare myself for the unknown. By the time I got to it, every fiber of my being was on hyperalert and my nerves were as tight as they could get. When it turned out to be just a violation, I finished what I needed to do then walked back to my vehicle. It was only when I was sitting in the seat of my cruiser that I actually relaxed, and then sometimes not until after the other vehicle pulled away."

A doctor in charge of an ER is on a coffee break when he's suddenly paged about an auto pileup; he may not know upon first communication how many patients he'll have. His adrenaline surge begins with that first call and doesn't stop until he knows that every patient has been taken care of, even if other doctors are assisting him.

A firefighter has the same adrenaline rush when the firehouse alarm rings.

EMS teams are fast on the scene, adrenaline pumping and ready for anything.

In all these instances, the adrenaline gland is pumping; the senses are registering during hyperalertness. All will experience a state of helplessness when someone is hurt or dies. And all will rethink the incidents in their heads over and over again to see what they could have done differently to change the outcome. The one thought going through the heads of all those saving lives is no different from the thought going through a soldier's head. "God, please let me and my training succeed."

A flashback will come unexpectedly because the PTSD victim often won't know or remember all that was heard, smelled, seen, felt, or tasted. At least two physical senses are needed to imprint a trauma, yet any *one* of the five remembered senses can trigger a flashback, forcing the victim to relive the past incident. This is why PTSD victims seek places where they can be by themselves or with an understanding partner. They try to eliminate any stimuli they think will trigger a flashback. They feel helpless enough being on display to others during a flashback.

Also, there's the mistrust issue. Because they don't have control in their lives, they must maintain control wherever and whenever they can. They can't allow others to see their weakness or give anyone anything that can be used against them. In the head of every flashback victim is the thought, "Is someone going to take advantage of me while I'm in another reality?"

Several years ago, I had wondered why two men could go to war and one would come back diagnosed with PTSD and the other not. I talked with Viet Nam veterans about their childhood backgrounds and what experiences they'd had since then. I came to this conclusion.

A soldier *not* diagnosed PTSD either had a relatively normal childhood (if anyone can truly define normal for me); or, if he had been traumatized in his youth, he had been given the tools to deal with the trauma, or someone outside the home had helped him. If the war is the soldier's first trauma, he might be stable enough to deal with the nightmares or memories of the war. Any soldier having to go to war should be encouraged to write down experiences as soon as he gets back, in group support, if necessary. In truth, group support is preferable because of the impact that comes from sharing. One-on-one only contributes to the isolation.

Those who had been abused in childhood were generally the vets diagnosed with PTSD. With no tools after the first trauma, the soldier did the best (s)he could. By the time they went to 'Nam, their psyche already impaired and weakened, the sight of death, bombs blowing up comrades, the noise, and all the experiences of war created a PTSD victim.

There's no cure for PTSD because we can't cut out our memories.

Even though a blind person can't see, a deaf person can't hear, or a mute can't speak, fear can imprint the senses into their imaginations and into their memory banks. Fear, in any shape or thought, is the first emotion experienced in a state of *helplessness*, be it real or imagined. Fear of the unknown not only triggers the adrenaline gland, but also cements the fear into our psyche. The emotions involved in the fear of no control are synonymous to the emotions we would experience if we walked into a dark cave where things touch us, we hear noises, and odors conjure up images. With no sight, we are left with our imaginations, not to mention the other senses heightened with the loss of sight. When you walk out of that cave, you won't forget the emotional experience for a very long time.

The human mind is made up of the soul/higher self, the internal spiritual force within us; and the ego/psyche, the force that reacts to external stimuli. The bridge spanning or connecting these two ethereal elements is the brain, our bio-computer programmed since birth. As the brain cares for our body's functions and needs, it also translates the ego to the body, and the higher self to the body: i.e., when we are angry, it's the ego reacting; when we sit in prayer or meditation, the higher self calms us.

Picture a pendulum hanging from that bridge (brain). When traumatized, our psyche enters into chaos and the pendulum sways to the ego side, putting us out of balance. If we experience a lot of abuse without tapping into the nurturing side of ourselves, the pendulum swings farther to the chaos side, taking our bio-computer with it. Hence, stress, illness, strong negative emotions, anger, the need to self-medicate, etc.

In order to come into balance after the trauma, we need to swing the pendulum back toward the soul part that is the love and nurturing aspect of our being. We need to share the trauma, hear soothing words, be touched and/or caressed affectionately, and be made to feel loved. These elements are needed to reverse the imprint of the event and make it a life-experience lesson that will empower us, and no longer a trauma that will disempower us.

An external trauma needs to be balanced with the same physical senses it took to create the trauma before it was set into the psyche. Dictated by the way we are feeling on the inside—the *within* reacting to the *without*—you treat the trauma with gentleness and love to balance the violence it took to imprint it. This is not being mushy. This is, in fact, instilling a concept usually missing from the individual's life from the beginning. Had the principles of love been in place from infancy, the tools necessary to deal with a trauma would more than likely have also been in place. Once there is an understanding through compassion stemming from love, the *without* will react to the higher self of the *within*.

When an herbalist creates a healing formula, she will use three ingredients: an herb to handle the problem; an herb to clean up the path as the first herb does its healing; and an herb to soothe the path behind herbs one and two. I have used this formula psychologically with my clients. One, we take care of the present anxiety before journaling back to the original hurt. Two, we connect the dots as we move forward from the original trauma to the present. Three, I incorporate rehabilitation by teaching self-love and redirecting some of their social behaviors, always with their permission.

As a rule, when the trauma existed in the client's youth, the family involved was dysfunctional, from ignorance, to illiteracy, to alcoholism, or drug abuse; and the adults involved would have created their own social values and behaviors. Once a client heals the trauma and becomes independent, (s)he understands why some of their previous behaviors will not be acceptable in a society in which they wish to elevate themselves.

Just teaching our teenage foster children how to use a seven-piece silverware setting at a table took them out of the McDonald Syndrome of plastic ware, paper cups, and Styrofoam containers. Sitting at a table with real place settings and cloth napkins, conversing with other adults while soft music played in the background, gave all of them the confidence to expand themselves into other avenues of social functions. It never ceased to amaze me how such a small act in the social graces gave those kids such courage.

In dealing with my clients, I use elements not common in most practices. I hug or touch the individual: i.e., touching the arm or shoulder, or actually hugging them. Because it isn't common, we discuss touch at the beginning just so there's an understanding and that it isn't a license to take a liberty. Sometimes I've even tousled a grown man's hair and was immediately surprised with a child's *aw shucks* demeanor. Appropriate, affectionate touch is an element missing in the lives of most abused children. There's also the element of proof. If touch feels that good, what else can they be missing in relation to self-love and loving others?

People tend to push their children out the door as fast as they can. And once the child goes out the door, the parent stops teaching. Though they will respond when the child acts up or out, or when someone complains, they usually let the teachers or other caregivers do the teaching, or let the child fend for itself as best as (s)he can.

I think it's curious that *all* teachers and educators are not allowed to hug the children because a *few* people sexually abuse children. A teacher's hug may be the only kind touch a child receives. Instead, why not teach children what an inappropriate touch is and why they shouldn't allow it? Also, teach them that an abuser will orally threaten them to control and manipulate them, or to simply keep them quiet. Teach children to tell a teacher or a trusted adult when they have been touched inappropriately. Educate children on what might happen and what to do about it rather than waiting until their ignorance and fears allow them to be traumatized by an abuser. We don't give our children enough credit for their intelligence or sensibility.

After giving my clients permission to love themselves and

showing them how it's done throughout the therapy sessions, I enjoy watching how fast their psyche heals in the light of knowledge. It's much like watching a rose open its petals in the sunlight. More importantly, I know how well they're learning their lessons of self-love by how much of their inner child they recapture and bring back into their lives.

It's difficult to imagine a counselor saying, "I love you." But there needs to be an understanding about basic human needs. One cannot obtain healing at the core level, or even peace of mind, when there are low self-esteem issues, and these issues stem from the lack of love. When someone has been abused in childhood, (s)he allowed the abuse because (s)he had never received the tools needed to understand abuse or prevent it; these tools are taught or administered through and from love. When someone doesn't feel loved, their low self-esteem assumes they deserve abuse.

Self-love is not defined as being self-centered or providing only for ourselves by putting ourselves first. It's defined through the understanding that we are gifts from God/Goddess and that we should love ourselves as God/Goddess loves us. I think it interesting that we are born not loving ourselves; that we need to be taught self-love. Only through loving and understanding ourselves from this perspective can we, with compassion and without thought, love another.

The foundation of love is respect or honor. This applies to a pet, a house, a spouse, a friend, to anything or anyone with which or with whom you have a relationship. To honor a person or a thing is to accept them for whatever or whomever for whatever they are, including their faults. And therein lays the key word—faults. It's difficult for us to look at faults in others and accept them. Faulty things as gifts from God are not usually what we have in mind, as we are raised to believe that anything related to God is perfect. More often than not, we are hurting too much to accept something as faulty as ourselves. We need something stronger or better, more than we are. How can we look up to someone on our same level?

When the three principles of healing are applied, and the therapist and the client are using their integrity, and the psyche is allowed to look back and reason with the past, one does heal. I have never seen it fail. How can it? One thing my foster teenagers taught me is that we humans are full of behavior patterns that are always linked to an original trauma.

Does one heal one hundred percent? You can't fight a war and come out of it unscathed. You will have your scars, be they physical, emotional, or mental; I have never heard of a spiritual scar. But you can put your flashbacks where they belong. You can come to terms with your abusers, with those you feel have done you wrong, and you can even get past your friend's dead body, if that's what's needed. Everything can come to closure once you understand.

Frances Bacon said, "Knowledge is power," and he said a mouthful.

You can come to peace with your past.

✻

Survivor Psalm

I have been victimized.
I was in a fight that was
not a fair fight.
I did not ask for the fight.
I lost.
There is no shame in losing
such fights.
I have reached the stage of
survivor and am no longer a
slave of victim status.
I look back with sadness
rather than hate.
I look forward with hope
rather than despair.
I may never forget, but I need
not constantly remember.
I was a victim.
I am a survivor.

Gift From Within
www.GiftFromWithin.org

Epilogue

I am content.

The wind can still make me blush. I thank the trees for their coolness as I work in my gardens during the heat of the day, creating flower beds *without and within me* in a way that would make the little woman proud. I remembered her after my auto accident and was ashamed for having forgotten her. However, retrospection of my life shows that I have not forgotten what she had taught me.

My past is in its place, and I have healed as much as one can expect. I have not had a flashback in a year and that one was a minor one, surprising as it was. At this point, I don't really think the big ones will come back. I know they're back there, in the recesses of my memory bank where the rest of them are; and, I can see the images. Large groups of people are still an issue if the noise level is at a certain pitch. I also need space because I can't take being crowded. Sometimes Wal-Mart is just too large or too much. And some nights I don't sleep, but that might be post-menopausal. I still jump at noises and have some trust issues. Just because I've healed from my past doesn't mean I'm ready to jump into anything.

My memory has a hitch in its get-along. That means I can be relating something and a word in my head will disappear. I just wait a moment until my memory takes its step, hitches up again, then the word comes back and I can get along with what I was saying. Folks are patient. Sometimes I misspeak, but that's okay, too. The correction comes.

The people in my community have allowed me to gift them with what talents I can now use, though I do make mistakes. They have embraced me for who I am, without explanation. I don't feel I owe them anything, but because of my love for them, I shall give to my communities of residence, church, and neighbors in any capacity my abilities will allow.

I am not looking forward to going "out there" because I feel I have finally found a home, and I'm no longer hurting. But, as a survivor, coupled with the love for (Wo)Man, Guidance has directed me to do my share to help those who have the desire and the courage to walk their paths back home as I have done.

I ask for no judgment, advice, or sympathy. However, I'll take all sincere hugs. If leaving out any part of my life experiences, no matter how horrific, would have made me less than who I am today, given a choice, I would choose to walk through it again. I'm relearning who I am and trying to rehabilitate into the person I wish to become. I love my *self* and all of Creator's children, and harbor no ill will toward anyone. I choose with whom I spend my time, including my extended family members.

With your permission, I wish to share one more story with you. I have told parts of it to a few people, but I'll share the entire episode here.

Several weeks after my flashback, I walked out the back door of the dome, past the studio, up the hill above the dome, and sat down by a huge oak tree. I had no idea where I was going until I saw the tree; and I had never sat next to it before. Though a magnificent tree, it hadn't earned a second thought.

Since the flashback, I had been crying like an open faucet and hadn't been able to shut off the tears. I don't know how long I sat against the oak tree and cried my *soul tears*. I had once cried for death and it didn't work, so I figured it wasn't an option. But I was so depressed I was beyond hurting. Everything within me had culminated into one huge pain, and I hoped that sitting by the grand oak and just letting it all out would stop the flood of tears or; at the very least, shrink the pain down to a bearable size.

I closed my eyes and sat there, waiting for God only knew what. I had meditated before and always experienced activity before moving into the light. But this time, it began differently. I didn't start out in the dark and travel to the light. I started in the blackest black that could be seen, though I certainly couldn't see anything, and there I remained. After what I determined to be a few minutes, the blackness began to move in a very subtle swaying motion. Slowly, ever so slowly, I sensed my body move from a sitting position to a reclining position, as though sitting sideways in a chair or being held in someone's arms. It had the same feel as a flashback, my sitting beside the tree yet lying in a sideways position, but it had softness to it, nothing negative or hurtful.

I just sat there and swayed as though I was barely swinging on a swing. It took a moment or two more to realize the sensation of my being in an envelope, or a blanket, or gigantic arms—it can't be described. I felt like I was being held. I don't remember when I stopped crying. I felt a slow heartbeat, coming up from a great depth. Within a few moments *my* heartbeat matched its rhythm. Something akin to a feather barely kissed my face, and I smelled fragrances of vanilla extract and exotic perfume.

I didn't hurt anymore.

As I sat there swaying, I heard whispers from out of the depths of the embracing womb, seemingly coming from every direction at the same time. The chanted murmurs, barely audible, grew louder. As each syllable of the chant penetrated my body, my cells absorbed the sounds and resonated as each murmur grew in pitch. When my cells felt full, I heard four words as my brain registered accompanying visions: I understood where the wind begins; how the Earth Mother moves; where my existence is in the universe; and why we never die.

I don't know how much time passed but coming out of the meditation, my brain and my body moved slowly, and I found myself leaning against the tree as though someone had picked me up and laid me against the trunk of the oak. My pain came back, and in that instant, and *only* in that very instant, I understood that we create our own emotional and mental pain, with the help of our ego.

Those four words carried me through the next four years and

to the end of this book, and they will carry me through to the end of my earthly life. I end my e-mails with these four words. I embrace as many people as I can and repeat these four words in their ear. If you sit and meditate on these four words, you can receive an iota of what I experienced. I wish to leave you with the same four words I received:

Know You Are Loved

Acknowledgments

I wish to thank the following: My husband for his stubbornness; Genie Cass for always believing in me; Ruth Crawford, LCSW, for her honest, gentle therapy at the VA and for writing the introduction to this book; Joyce Rawlings-Davies for teaching me that it's okay to get close to a friend, and for encouraging me when I wanted to just ditch it all and hide; Karen Fredette for allowing me to display my life and heart in a loving atmosphere without saying "poor baby;" the Ladies Book Club and Vigilante Committee (Ladies, when you come together, you have a beautiful power that equals none other); my church family for watching over me from the beginning and helping me in my healing and growth; Irene Libretto, LCSW, also a PTSD survivor, for keeping me encouraged; Dr. Terry Apt, ARNP-C, N.D. (Girlfriend, had it not been for you, this book would have gotten lost); my editor, Sharon K. Garner, an author in her own right, for sticking with it and making sure I came across coherent; Jamie Saloff for guiding me into creating my own publishing company and putting together this book—it has been a pleasurable experience; and Peggy DeBell, a photo-textile artist, for doing her level best to make me look good.

I wish to also extend my heartfelt gratitude to our foster children for allowing me to love them; our son for adopting us; to all those who have contributed in their own way, through gifts of encouragement, prayers, lending an ear, a hand, or a hug; and to Anne Castle for teaching me how to communicate with nonspeaking Alzheimer's patients. If I have forgotten to thank anyone, please forgive me and remember I am PTSD.

I would also like to acknowledge all those I have counseled in the past. Please, know that I've cried as you cried, and grew as you grew. You have helped me to put pain into words; know that others will benefit from your tears and growth.

Last, but not least, I wish to thank Guidance for being there throughout my life and for giving me the greatest gift of all—me.

Peace with PTSD

Peace with PTSD, a non-profit, was created for the purpose of abuse/PTSD victims and their families. Our website, **www.PeaceWithPTSD.org**, and our quarterly newsletter, *Peace with PTSD*, hopefully debuting spring, 2008, will be created by the readers. We will research; gather information from across the country for support groups; other healing modalities; and share what has worked and has not worked with other abuse/PTSD victims, using their words and resources.

I wish to connect the abuse/PTSD community and offer a place for them to share and still keep their anonymity. Abuse/PTSD victims sometimes feel they are alone but, at the same time, are very cautious about support groups.

Please visit our website at **www.PeaceWithPTSD.org** to contact us or email the author at: **lady@peacewithptsd.org,** and let us know what you wish to see on the website and in the newsletter. We also welcome professionals who wish to help this community of people with their insights. We welcome all of you to share our space.

Printed in the United States
92168LV00004B/130-132/A

9 780979 888304